MW00344762

Get Ready

For Your Best Marriage Now

A Transformative Book for Couples

Rick Thomas

The Counseling Solutions Group, Inc.

Copyright

Dedication

To Lucia

Endorsements

"Marriage is not just a fun joyride but something that should take time, reflection, and good question asking that allows Christ's light to shine for His magnificent purpose and glory. Rick has masterfully provided just the book for any couple—dating, engaged, or married—to address areas where we all struggle or sin.

You will not be left feeling directionless, guilted, or shamed but instead met with grace, humility, gentleness, and truth written in love with what God's Word says and how His gospel redeems."

Sarah Lange, RN, Homemaker, Biblical Counseling Ministry Leader at Imago Dei Church, Milwaukee, WI

"Rick Thomas has crafted another excellent resource with *Get Ready:For Your Best Marriage Now*. This book is a relational masterpiece for those in any phase of dating, pre-engagement, engagement, or marriage.

Rick emphasizes the need to equip couples by following Christ's model of disciple making, training the whole person to be a thoroughly equipped man or woman. I have personally benefited from the material and the relational writing style Rick uses in this book. Truth balanced by love and compassion is the foundation on which *Get Ready* is based. Practical information and thought-provoking questions at the end of each chapter provide the reader with an application of the contents. This book will be a new addition to our pre-marital counseling resource list."

Julie Ganschow, Director and Biblical Counselor, Reigning Grace Counseling Center and author of *"Living Beyond the Heart of Betrayal: Biblically Addressing the Pain of Sexual Sin."*

"Rarely do we have a resource that speaks so well to both dating couples and married couples in one book. Rick has done just that in this book, *Get Ready*. It is filled with practical, relevant and biblical exercises that can be used effectively for both groups. It walks through how to have a biblical marriage that is centered on the gospel while addressing many struggles couples find themselves.

I appreciate the time Rick took to unpack the sexual issues that affect marriage with clarity, insight and biblical precision and where they stem from, but then also provides a right way of walking through that struggle to a place of greater oneness in the relationship.

If you are a counsellor, pastor, or one who walks alongside others, you will want this book. It will be an asset to every counsellor who works with married couples and with those preparing to be married.

It will become a part of my pre-marriage counselling without a doubt but will also be used again and again with wives and husbands. I have used Rick's timely blogs as homework assignments for years and having all of this in one book is a welcome help!"

Karen Gaul, Biblical counsellor, Southern Ontario. ACBC Certified, BA Biblical Counseling, Trinity Theological Seminary, Indiana. GraceBiblicalCounselling.Net

"*Get Ready*! Rick Thomas's newest book is full of God's grace, but it is also hard-hitting as it addresses premarital/marital issues that the prudish might consider taboo. Rick does not desire to shock the reader though. Rather, he understands from both Scripture and his many years of counseling that foundational issues of marriage are avoided too often until marital crises force couples to begin these important discussions. But at that point in relationships, sadly, it is often too late.

Get Ready is written to address common issues that will likely occur as two sinners are united in covenant marriage and to address these issues before they become problems which destroy intimacy and hinder relationship with God. What I appreciated most about this book is that it is both a theology of marriage as well as a tool to enable conversations and practical applications within a couple's relationship.

Rick skillfully supplies couples and counselors with hundreds of questions that need to be carefully considered and answered honestly by each couple. If you or someone you know is about to be married or if you engage in premarital and marital biblical counseling, then I highly recommend that you purchase Rick Thomas's upfront, new resource: *Get Ready*."

Dr. Daniel R. Berger II, Author, Speaker, and Director of Alethia International Ministries

"As a pastor and counselor, I am constantly on the lookout for resources that can help me to assist people seeking aid in relationships and their marriages. *Get Ready* does this in a very thoughtful way by looking at the issues, from premarital dating to deep relational hurts, identifying the root cause of marital problems.

In an easy to read format, Rick's examination takes the biblical route to the heart of the couple. His message helps couples to see that the heart is where problems originate. The book is thoroughly biblical while exceptionally practical. *Get Ready* is a collection of wisdom that every discerning pastor or counselor will want on his shelf."

Dr. Mark Schmitz, Director of SoulCareNC Counseling, Hickory, NC, Pastor, East Hickory Church, Hickory, NC

"*Get Ready* should be required reading for any couple considering marriage! There's no fluff when it comes to Rick Thomas's writing. He's candid (yet gracious) when it comes to the kind of questions we should be asking ourselves and each other—something that may feel awkward to start with but is so important to the success of our lives individually and as couples.

He is humble in his examples, and his heart is to genuinely want the best for each individual, knowing the reality of what comes after marriage, which is a lot more challenging than we imagine when in the dating season.

As he points out, our primary concern should be our relationship with God; if that's right, then our relationships with each other will be much less bumpy! As always, Rick includes many questions to ask ourselves in his "Call to Action" sections where what he shares can be applied to our lives.

My recommendation is to take what he says very seriously and don't gloss over any concerns you have in your relationship. It's much better to be honest, ask the questions, and deal with them appropriately in advance of marriage. If you are already married, find help now before things get worse."

Demelza Marie, Media Ministry and Entrepreneur

"Rick has a way with his writing of getting to the point of Scripture application in a deep and really practical way. So is the case with this look at marriage preparation. He takes us on an awesome look into the Scriptures regarding relationships moving toward marriage, but these thoughts also keenly apply to current marriages.

What makes Rick's books stand out is the way he presses us, the readers, to slow down and thoughtfully apply truths to our lives. Foundational to marriage and cutting against the grain of so many marriage books today, Rick takes us to Genesis 1–3 in a beautifully unique way, helping us see that being made in God's image shows that Adam needed Eve to reflect the community, Trinitarian nature of God fully.

He didn't need her love or respect. Instead, God created her to complete this image of God's picture fully. What follows is a deeper look at God's design of marital function. *Get Ready* isn't a book of self-help but of God-exalting Scripture application. Work through this book whether married or not!"

Derek Black, MA Biblical Counseling, Pastor of Acts 247 Recovery Church, Soldotna, AK

Table of Contents

Introduction

How to Use This Book

If you are thinking about dating, courtship, or getting married, this could be the most important book you'll ever read. I realize what I just wrote may come across as an overstatement or hyperbolic marketing, but it is not. I have been in the counseling "business" for many years, and the most common situation I have counseled are marriages in trouble. These troubled marriages did not just happen. The problems in any marriage are rooted in the two people who are married before they were married.

It can be a challenge for a person to see future marriage problems with their current dating partner. This blind spot is why I wrote this book. I'm not trying to talk you out of dating or getting married. My goals are to come alongside you to help bring more clarity to how you think about (1) dating, (2) the person you are dating, and (3) what your future could look like with the person you are dating.

What you see is not what you're going to get. Once you're married, the real person whom you married will be more apparent than you had ever imagined. I hope this book will help you to see what you may not be able to see right now and to know how God can give you courageous favor to do the right things. For you to get the most out of this book, my suggestive devotional assignments are as follows:

1. God – Take all the questions in this book to your "closet" and talk to God about them. There are more than 250 questions throughout this book.
2. Bible – Research, read, and reflect upon all the Scriptures included in this book.
3. Self – Write out your answers. Be specific. Be vulnerable. Be practical.
4. Situations – Ask God to let whatever your life situation is to be a means of grace to change you.
5. Others – Invite a courageous, competent, and compassionate friend into your life by sharing what you and God discuss as you read and reflect upon this book.

It's a Workbook

This book is the culmination of thousands of hours of counseling with marriages that came to me because they either did not know the content of this book, did not know how to apply it, or refused to use what they knew. All of their marriages were in trouble, and they hoped to reverse years of poor decision-making and relational conflict.

What you are about to read has been field tested. It will work for you in proportion to your willingness to take it to heart while practically applying it to your life and relationship. I recommend that you read this book slowly, reflectively, prayerfully, and conversationally. You may want to read it more than once. This book is not meant to be read and shelved. It is a reusable tool that will never wear out no matter how many times you use it. Do not be afraid: use it often.

At the end of each chapter, I have "call to action" opportunities that are meant to probe your thought life as well as your practical experience. Ask the Spirit of God to open your eyes to see any hidden things. Ask Him to give you the courage to change what needs changing, no matter how hard it feels at the moment. And above all else, expect God's favor on your life as you humbly submit to His guidance while you move through this resource.

If You Are Married

This book is for you, too. Perhaps your marriage has hit the rocks. After years of muddling through, you feel as though you've lost all hope. Your hope is not lost. I wrote this book for people who want a great marriage. The content applies (1) to those who have yet to tie the knot, (2) to those who have tied the knot, and (3) to those who have untied the knot.

Whether pre-married, married, or post-married, the content of this book is about how to have a God-glorifying and mutually enjoyable marriage. If that is what you want, this is what you need. Don't be discouraged; be hopeful. God is a Healer of the hurting. If you are one of the hurting ones because your marriage went to the wrong place, I appeal to you to set aside some time to read this resource.

Find a friend to walk with you through it. Ask the Father to restore the brokenness. Expect His mercy and favor. I do not know if the Lord can transform your marriage, but I do know He can make your life better than what it is. The content in this book can assist you in that beautiful cause.

Rick
Greenville, SC

Chapter 1

The Decision

I said to my friend that when deciding anything, it is critical that you are "in faith" regarding that decision, which is why the most important question you will ever ask yourself when making a decision is, "Am I in faith to do what I want to do?" My friend responded by asking what I meant when I say that you "must be in faith" before you can move forward with a decision.

"But whoever has doubts is condemned if he eats, because the eating is not from faith. For whatever does not proceed from faith is sin" (Romans 14:23).

The term "in faith" comes from Paul's language in Romans 14:23. He was saying that all of our decisions must go forth from a heart of faith. Maybe a few synonyms will help you to bring more color to the word faith: trust, belief, hope, or confidence. Here are a few sample questions to ask yourself when working through the process of biblical decision-making. You'll notice how they are five ways of asking the same thing.

- Are you in faith to proceed in marriage?
- Are you trusting the Lord to proceed forward with marriage?
- Do you believe marrying this person is the right thing for you?
- Is your hope in the Lord as you move forward with marriage?

Is your confidence resting in the Lord, which releases you to proceed in marrying this person?

All of these questions are similar in that they are asking this one thing: are you in faith to get married? I chose to use the term "in faith" because it is how Paul appealed to the Romans to think about their decision-making. My friend was in the process of deciding to marry someone. His potential decision is why I asked him if he was "in faith" to move forward—to proceed with marrying his girlfriend. I wanted to know if he was confident that God wanted him to do that.

We spent the next hour or so unpacking how to grow in faith while addressing some of the ancillary pitfalls to biblical decision-making. While I cannot recreate that discussion in its totality here, I do want to present some of the most critical points that we discussed, which are essential for any couple thinking about marriage.

Case Study: Making a Decision

Biff and Mable are thinking about marriage. I asked Biff if he was in faith for this new adventure with a new bride. The life of a Christian is born out of and proceeds from a life of faith (Romans 1:17; Hebrews 11:6).

- Our decision to trust God is by faith.
- Our decision to marry is by faith.
- Our decision to eat at that (restaurant) is by faith.
- Our decision to not sin is by faith: you believe it is wrong to (insert the sin here).

In the context of this discussion on decision-making, being "in faith" means that what you are doing is the right thing for you to do. It implies that you are confident the Lord wants you to do what you are about to do. This kind of decision-making applies to the simplest things in life as well as to the more complex decisions you must make to live well in God's world.

Biff and Mable's decision is one of those more complex choices in life. Participating in the interactive adventure of marriage is one of the top three things we do. Family, work, and church are the three spheres where most Christians spend the bulk of their lives. You will not wrestle as much about whether you should eat at McDonald's, Burger King, or have a meal at home, but you will spend considerably more time trying to be confident that your future spouse is the one you believe God wants you to marry.

Four-Legged Decision

Faith is like a stool upon which you sit. That stool has four legs: canon, community, conscience, and Comforter. If you place yourself in a context where these four means of grace give you sound advice, you will probably be safe to move forward with what you want to do.

- Canon – What does the Bible say about getting married? (2 Timothy 3:16–17)
- Community – What do a few trusted, courageous, and wise friends say about you marrying this person? (Proverbs 11:14)
- Conscience – What do you think about getting married to this person? (Romans 2:14–15)
- Comforter – What does the Spirit of God say about you marrying? (John 16:13)

Most poor decisions happen because the person who made the decision was not benefiting from these four powerful means of grace the Lord provides for us. They either did not know about this process, or, even more sinister, they did not want to hear

23

what God and others had to say to them. One of the marks of humility is when a person will hold their ideas loosely while submitting them to God's Word as well as to His community for more careful analysis.

This worldview reminds me of a time when I became angry at my daughter. After I lashed out at her, and after she had slithered back to her room, I asked Lucia if she felt that I was too harsh with her. I was not asking because I was humble. I was asking, hoping that Lucia would side with my evil motives by saying that I was not unkind to our daughter. The truth was that I did not want to know the truth. I was hoping to be justified in my sin. Mercifully, Lucia did not side with my sinister motives, but she admonished me in a loving but firm way by saying I was wrong in the way I treated our child.

I suppose there are times when we know what we should do, but we don't want to do it (James 4:17). We can be so deceptive that we do not want to submit our ideas to others because they may not side with us. We can be even more deceptive when we present our thoughts to individuals whom we know will not have the courage or the wisdom to counter what we want. We pick certain people who have no potential or courage to offer an alternate opinion.

Such a person is not looking for God's thoughts on the matter. They are seeking a way to justify what they have already determined to do, and they go the extra mile by finding people who agree with them.

Distancing Yourself from Truth

This deception has immediate and long-term results. The direct result is that you can get what you want. The long-term effects are twofold: (1) The outcome will not be as you hoped, and your unwillingness to cooperate with God will complicate your life when inevitable disappointment comes. (James 4:6 – God resists the proud.) (2) If you continue to deceive people to accomplish your selfish goals, you will eventually harden your conscience, which will make it more difficult in the future for you to perceive God's truth and direction for your life (Hebrews 3:7–8).

Individuals who want to manipulate people and situations rarely consider this second point because they want to fulfill their desires. They do not understand that when you alter God's truth, there is a proportional adverse effect on the conscience (Romans 1:18).

The conscience is our "moral thermostat" that God gave to us to alert us of right and wrong. Even the non-Christian has this gift from the Lord (Romans 2:14–15). Problems happen when we tweak our moral thermostats through justifications, rationalizations, or blame-shifting—the three main ways we alter God's truth. As we do this, it creates a hardening effect on the conscience (1 Timothy 4:2).

- Justification – Pronouncing my actions as not guilty, regardless of what the Bible says about them.
- Rationalization – Comparing what I did with others by minimizing the wrongness, while creating tolerance for doing what I want to do.
- Blaming – Rather than perceiving and acknowledging my wrongness, I blame others for what went wrong: I refuse to own my sin.

If your conscience, like a thermostat, is altered, it will not give you an accurate reading. It may be 100 degrees in your home, but the thermostat says everything is fine. A conscience manipulated is worse than useless. It's dangerous. The more you mute your conscience, the more distance you will put between (1) yourself,

(2) God's Word, (3) His community, and (4) the Spirit's illuminating power. You will become more and more isolated from the truth with no inner voice to persuade you otherwise.

- Canon – Will you humbly seek God's Word to find the answers to your questions about marriage?
- Community – Will you humbly place your marriage desires in the hands of trusted, wise, and courageous friends who will not automatically tell you what you want to hear?
- Conscience – Will you not only listen to what your conscience is telling you, but will you respond to it—assuming your conscience is in line with God's Word?
- Comforter – Will you honestly say you have not exchanged the truth of God for a lie because you have submitted your desires for marriage to scrutiny through the means of the canon of God's Word, the community of God's children, your conscience, and the Holy Spirit?

"Therefore God gave them up in the lusts of their hearts to impurity, to the dishonoring of their bodies among themselves, because they exchanged the truth about God for a lie and worshiped and served the creature rather than the Creator, who is blessed forever! Amen" (Romans 1:24).

Expect Disappointment

One of the more instructive things I have seen about decision-making is that after we make a decision and proceed in faith, we forget to factor in future disappointment. It is like we don't remember how our lives are calls to suffer (1 Peter 2:21). You may recall that on a dark and stormy night, the Lord asked Peter to step off a boat and walk on water. Peter did as he was asked to do (Matthew 14:28–36). He stepped off the vessel and proceeded in faith, probably believing it was going to turn out well for him.

After Peter had walked a few steps on the water, he began to notice the waves and the wind. He quickly forgot who called him, as his faith shifted from the Lord to the waves. What he could see and experience was more influential to him than the Lord (2 Corinthians 5:7). Aren't we like this? We pray. We seek counsel. We move forward in faith. Then all hell breaks loose, and we lose faith for the process. That is what the Lord rebuked Peter for after they returned to the safety of the boat: "O you of little faith, why did you doubt?" (Matthew 14:31).

Let me go ahead and state the obvious here: no matter what your decision is after you move forward with your plans, you will be disappointed in some way, whether small or large. One of the more recurring applications of the gospel is how the Lord uses the process of dying to ourselves to accomplish His purposes in our lives and relationships (Matthew 16:24–26; 2 Corinthians 1:8–9). At times we can think more like spoiled, first-world people than like Christians. We embrace the happily-ever-after worldview, which is right in a sense: we will be happy forever in eternity (Revelation 21:4), but that is not our reality for the here and now.

If you smuggle in the notion that your decision to marry someone is more about your happiness than God's glory, you will surely be set up for disappointment. Plus, you will live in doubt, regret, bitterness, and anger as you think about your past decisions. Self-preservation must not be the driving theme of your decision-making. While you should not be foolish by blindly jumping off a cliff, you must not err the other way by trying to insulate all your decisions from potential suffering.

Purposeful Freedom

Sometimes God gives us multiple options to choose from, none of which are necessarily wrong. It might not be wrong to eat at McDonald's or Burger King or home. Decision-making does not have to be like an archer standing 100 yards from a target with one arrow trying to hit the bull's eye. If you follow the steps outlined in this chapter, you may come to the end of the process with multiple choices from which to choose to be your future mate.

Maybe you want to go on a vacation, and you land on two options: the mountains or the beach. Perhaps there are two potential marriage partner options. They both fit within the four-legged stool metaphor:

- Canon – The Bible does not prohibit either one.
- Community – Your close friends weigh-in, and they see no problem with either one.
- Conscience – Your conscience is free on the matter.
- Comforter – It appears there is no quenching or grieving of the Spirit with either choice (Ephesians 4:10; 1 Thessalonians 5:19).

In such a situation as this, you are free to choose one or the other. In the case of a vacation, you may want to do both—an option that is not available when selecting a mate. You should not sweat your decision. Be free. Where sin is not involved, choose while rejoicing in God's kindness to give you more than one option. Just before I met Lucia, I had gone out with another girl. Suddenly, I had two girls in my life. After going through this process, it proved how it was not wrong to continue seeing either one of them. Then I made a fabulous choice.

Call to Action

1. Are you sure the Lord wants you to marry that person?
2. Are you holding your desires for marriage loosely while submitting them to others?
3. Do you want to know the truth, and are you humbly seeking answers—specifically from competent people, who do not always agree with you?
4. Is your motive for marriage more about God's glory than selfish desires? How do you know?
5. How much does self-protection or self-preservation influence your decision-making? How much does foolish thinking impact your decision to marry?

To the Premarital Counselor

There is one question that transcends all other matters in premarital counseling. It is this: "Are you sure, confident, or in faith that you are to marry this person?" The reason that question is the most important one that you can ask is that there will come a time in this couple's future marriage when bad things will happen to them.

- They may lose their home.
- They may lose a job.
- They may become bankrupt.
- They may develop a lifetime disability.
- They may discover a spouse is hiding a life-dominating sin.
- They may have a miscarriage.
- They will learn hurtful things about their spouse that they did not know while dating.
- They will become older.
- They will change.

- They will not be the same people that they were while dating.

There may be a time when most of the reasons they had for their marriage and the things they liked about being married go away. If that is the case, there must be one thing left on the table: they believed God wanted them to marry each other.

It is essential that all premarital counseling walks through this concept of biblical decision-making while exploring the couple's reasons, motives, and agendas for marriage. They will more than likely tell you that they are in faith to move forward to matrimony. Do not be deterred: you must explore their motives and reasons. The couple must know that being married to each other is the right thing to do, or as Paul said, they must move forward in faith.

Chapter 2

Your Need

Let's pretend there were only two chapters in the Bible—the first two. Let's pretend your name is Adam, and all you know is what's happening in Genesis one and two. There is no fall, no sin, no needs, no wants, no gospel, and no need for an incarnate Christ. It is a beautiful world with you and Creator God (Genesis 2:7). It is hard for us to think what it would have been like for Adam because we live in a post-Genesis three world (Genesis 3:6). We filter everything in the first two chapters of Genesis through a post-fall lens, a filter marred by sin (Romans 8:22).

It would be like standing in your living room looking through a dirty window at a beautiful day. The day is more beautiful than you could ever realize. Because of the stained window, it is hard to perceive or appreciate the beauty of what is on the other side. Even the things that we read in Genesis one and two are known through our tainted view of life because a fallen lens is the only lens we know.

Oh, to grasp what life must have been like for Adam in Genesis one and two. Yet, we must press on: we must seek to understand. There are conclusions to draw. For example, Adam lived in a perfect world. The perfection of God's creative work, in the beginning, is probably the most distinctive thing that separates how and where Adam lived with how and where we live. Our world is not perfect in any way, shape, or form.

Not only is our world broken, but so are our lives (Romans 3:10–12). Even being born a second time (John 3:7; 1 John 1:7–10) does not perfect us entirely. The theological term for our problem is total depravity, a condition that means no fiber of our being has been unaffected by sin.

Adam was not depraved like us. Sin had not yet affected him. He lived in perfect harmony with the Author of Shalom. It is crucial that we grasp the blessedness of Adam's life and experiences because how he lived is the only lens through which we can draw our best conclusions about Genesis 2:18.

Made in God's Image

"Then the LORD God said, 'It is not good that the man should be alone; I will make him a helper fit for him'" (Genesis 2:18).

The difference in how you read this verse depends on whether you are looking through a dirty window or a clean one. If you are interpreting Adam's situation through the lens of depravity, it would be easy to conclude that Adam was lacking and longing for more than what he had.

Most of us see Genesis 2:18 from our experience of loneliness, needs, longings, desires, and cravings. We upload Genesis 2:18 from a sin-centered, dirty-window perspective. We look back into the text while mapping our experience over it. Our experience is worlds away from where Adam was in the Garden of Eden. There was no sin in Adam or with Adam. The things that he thought, felt, and experienced were remarkably different from how you or I view, feel, and experience life.

It wasn't Adam who said he needed a companion, as though he experienced the incompleteness that we feel (Colossians

1:28). It was the Lord who said it was not right for him to be alone. It had not occurred to Adam that there was a problem with not having a wife since there was no such thing created at that time. This truth about Adam is where the saying "you can't know what you can't know" has an essential application. It reminds me of newly hatched ducks, and the first thing they see is a dog. What do they do? They follow the dog. The dog becomes the parent of the ducks.

The ducks don't have our knowledge so they're okay with following the dog. Adam was living large: he was benefiting from all that the Lord had created. He was living the dream. To speculate that Adam longed for someone or something that did not exist would be pushing the text too far. Adam was the hatched duckling. Life was good—according to him.

But the Lord was in creative mode. Only He knew what needed to happen next. Adam was not part of the decision-making committee (Genesis 1:26). His role was to be the happy recipient of whatever the Lord decided to bring his way. It is like the happy child who is not asking for anything but is gladly receiving whatever the parent brings home. Because Adam did not need Eve in the way that we think about companionship, it would be good to give more thought as to why the Lord gave Eve to Adam. The key here is to keep your mind in his world, rather than in yours.

"So God created man in his own image, in the image of God he created him; male and female he created them" (Genesis 1:27).

The Trinity made Adam in their image. That means they made Adam with the ability to image the many aspects of the Lord's character, e.g., holiness, love, patience, long-suffering, pity, and wisdom. This ability is amazing. He could do what nothing else in the Lord's creation could do. He could image God. Adam was able to be a reflection on earth of our good Lord in heaven. Of course, there was a slight problem. There were no options for him to do Trinitarian image-bearing. Having no community to image God was not good.

What We Need to Do

What Adam lacked was not someone to fill his empty love cup, but he needed someone who would allow him to put God entirely on display to the world. Adam was like the world's greatest baseball player with no place to play. He was suited up and equipped (in God's image), but he had no place to do the main thing that God had designed him to do. Adam did not need love, but he needed someone to be the recipient of his love. That is a significant distinction between the Genesis-one-and-two life and the Genesis-three life.

When Jesus talked about relationships in a perfect world, He did not talk about what we needed but about what we needed to do. For example, when He spoke about how to live out the Bible correctly, He said to love Him and to love others most of all (Matthew 22:36–40). The primary direction of God's love is always toward others, not toward ourselves (John 3:16). When Paul talked about Adam's relationship with Eve, He said that Adam should give his life for her (Ephesians 5:25). When Paul gave his version of the two great commandments, he stated that we should count others as more significant than ourselves (Philippians 2:3–4). He then tied that into what it means to have the mind of Christ (Philippians 2:5).

In a perfect world, we think about God and others more than ourselves. This concept is critical insight when we think about Adam's world. He did not need Eve as though there was something wrong with him. He needed Eve so that he could more

34

efficiently image the Person who had created him. Without Eve, Adam would have been missing out on an incredible privilege and opportunity, which was to magnify Creator God to the world.

Because Eve was made in the image of God and was without sin, she did not need Adam's love because there was nothing wrong with her either. She needed Adam for the same reason Adam needed her—to more efficiently image the One who had created her. That is essential thinking for any wife who wants to put God on display in her marriage.

Reversing the Effects of Sin

I suppose some women would read what I have said and say, "Praise God. Finally, somebody gets it. I hope my husband reads this and begins to give me what I need." That would be a post-Genesis-three worldview, the same perspective I have been trying to deconstruct. And, of course, the problem with us is that we live in a post-Genesis-three world where we see people as a means to satisfy our cravings rather than an opportunity to put God on display. Sin has a way of twisting every good thing the Lord has made by turning it onto ourselves.

Jesus came to untangle us from this kind of twisted thinking. He began the untangling process first by setting the example for how humanity is supposed to operate. He was our model for the non-needy life. He said, "For even the Son of Man came not to be served but to serve, and to give his life as a ransom for many" (Mark 10:45).

He gave His life and rose from the grave, which empowers us, the regenerated ones, to change our minds regarding how we think about God and others (Ephesians 4:22–24). Rather than using people for our purposes and perceived felt needs, we can now serve people. The gospel enables us to reverse the effects of sin. Through the power of the Spirit, we can strive to image God by being an encouragement and blessing to others rather than demanding others to serve us in whatever way we sinfully crave.

Adam did not say, "The Lord created you (Eve), so you could serve me." He did not live in a needy, "You must meet my expectations, or I am going to sin against you" world. Jesus, the last Adam, did not think that way either.

Living Like Our Leader

"Him we proclaim, warning everyone and teaching everyone with all wisdom, that we may present everyone mature in Christ" (Colossians 1:28).

As Christians, we have the power within us to stop demanding from others to give us what we want. Making demands on others to meet our needs is unregenerate, post-Genesis-three thinking that will not end well for anyone who attempts it. It takes faith in God to stop demanding from others to meet the brokenness that only the Lord can supply (Philippians 4:19). Living in a post-fall world makes for a natural temptation to seek post-fall solutions.

Our problem is that we are quicker to look for things in our world, especially from our friends and families, to fix our deepest longings rather than finding these longings satisfied through the means the Lord provides. It is like an addict trying to change herself through drugs. She will never be satisfied. She will never be content. She will always be needy. When others-centeredness turns into self-centeredness, a big black hole will open up and grow to infinite and insatiable proportions in our souls.

"The eye is not satisfied with seeing, nor the ear filled with hearing" (Ecclesiastes 1:8b).

The only way to experience transformation is through the counterintuitive means of the gospel, which is others-centered learning, loving, leading, and living. That is what the last Adam did when He lived among us (John 7:46). If you want to be happy and whole, the best thing you can do is to learn from Christ, the only person who lived sinlessly in a sinful world. He found fullness by giving, not by demanding others to meet His needs. He imaged God perfectly by putting the Father on display wherever He went. And like the first Adam, there were people available for Him to love. And He loved them well.

Jesus needed people because He needed to pour the love of God into them (1 John 4:8). Without somebody to love, how could any of us fully understand, experience, or image the Lord? I'm sure there are a few people in your life who could benefit from your image bearing. What if your reason for needing others was so that you could love them in a similar way that God loves you (Ephesians 5:1)?

- The Lord gave Adam somebody to love.
- The last Adam found people to love.
- Are you ready to love that way?

Call to Action

1. How does this teaching shape your motives for marriage?
2. What is the difference between marrying for your spouse to satisfy you versus marrying to please your spouse?
3. In what concrete and practical ways can God be put on display by the way you love your spouse (or future spouse)?
4. What have been the results of your expectations for others to satisfy your preferences, desires, or requests?
5. What areas of self-centeredness are still current in your former manner of life (Ephesians 4:22)?

6. Are you marrying to fill a void that only the Lord can fill?

Chapter 3

First Importance

One of the questions that I like to ask engaged couples is their reason for getting married. As you might imagine, the answers are all over the map. Here is a short list of some of the responses I have heard during premarriage counseling.

- I love him.
- We're in love.
- We have a lot in common.
- We are meant for each other.
- We're so different from each other.
- He treats me nice.
- It feels right.
- People have said that we're a perfect match.
- The Lord put us together.
- She's fun to be with.
- I like his personality.

All of these qualities and desires have merit, and each one is worth considering when thinking about the person you want to marry. With that said, to base your reasons for marriage on any of those things could be anywhere from insufficient to dangerous, depending on the couple. It is fair to say that every person who ever divorced had several of those things on their lists.

Then when things became complicated, their marriages were not able to survive. The growing list of stuff they did not like about each other overshadowed the stuff they did like about each other. This marriage problem happens because of the effect of sin in their lives and relationships. Though the Bible is clear that every person is a sinner (Romans 3:23), rarely do people have an adequate plan to fight the encroachments of sin (1 John 3:8), and the longer they stay together, the more their sinfulness will seek to defile each other.

Sin can overpower, alter, and even obliterate the good qualities you previously enjoyed about your spouse. That is why there must be a transcending quality in the person you're hoping to marry. A transcending quality is the only quality that will give you your best shot at persevering in a marriage covenant.

A Box of Chocolates

There is no way in the world for you to know what the person you want to marry will be like ten years from now, but there is one thing you can count on: the person you marry today will be different in a decade. All of us will regress into more self-centeredness, or we will progress into greater Christlikeness. The problem is that when a new couple first meets, they do not know which direction the other person is heading.

- Is he increasing in spiritual leadership?
- Is he decreasing in spiritual leadership?

The couple typically meets when they don't have much history. It's like being introduced to a new stock on the stock market. You don't know how it will trend. There is no history. Will this stock trend upward so you reap the benefits, or will it tank? The new couple begins building a unique history together: this is the dating season. Unfortunately, the dating season is, partially, an artificial period where the hope-filled couple tries hard to be nice to each other.

If the dating season lasts more than twelve months, they will begin to see authentic evidence of who they are. Of course, the problem here is that love can be blind, and when it comes to love, we tend to want to be blind. A bird in the hand is better than two in the bush. The dating couple is often too easily pleased with the bird they have in their grasp, even to the point of overlooking character deficiencies. Forrest Gump's analogy was correct: "Life is like a box of chocolates; you never know what you're going to get."

Spousal assessment is an opportunity that needs your attention. Some of the most religiously minded people married each other only to end their relationship in a bitter divorce. Then others folks began their covenant from a less desirable circumstance but experienced an incredible transformation by the grace of God. Thousands of preachers have miserable marriages, and thousands of non-ministry people have God-exalting, grace-empowered, mutually satisfying marriages. You can never fully know what you're going to get.

The initial criteria for assessing a person is too often inadequate, which is mystifying in light of what the Bible teaches us about the one transcending quality that will give you all you need to know to be married well.

The Main Thing

"So, whether you eat or drink, or whatever you do, do all to the glory of God" (1 Corinthians 10:31).

If the person whom you want to marry does not have as their primary mission in life the glory of God, you need to give long and sober consideration to the wisdom of marrying that person. But if the desire to glorify God is a person's passion, there is a good chance you could be in a meaningful and satisfying relationship with that person for the rest of your lives. There is nothing that transcends this God-centered quality, which means there is no sin, sinful desire, or sinful temptation that can overcome a person's dogged and steadfast determination to glorify God.

Whenever sin makes its advances, the desire to glorify God will eventually win the war against sin's intent. When Joseph was left alone in Potiphar's home, his master's wife began to put a move on the young slave. What she did not know was how the Lord had already captured the young man's affections. From his perspective, there was no way that he could sin against God.

"Now Joseph was handsome in form and appearance. And after a time his master's wife cast her eyes on Joseph and said, 'Lie with me.' But he refused and said to his master's wife, 'How then can I do this great wickedness and sin against God'" (Genesis 39:6b–10).

Joseph's primary intention in life was to spread the fame of God. He possessed a sober awareness of God's glory. He revered the Lord. A desire to magnify God through his miserable slave life consumed him (Psalm 34:3). If you are looking to make a covenant with a "Joseph-type person," that is your best play. It will not keep you from future heartbreak, but there is not a piece of information out there that is more affirming than a person's authentic and measurable desire to glorify God.

Paul said that no matter what you did, your primary goal must be to glorify God. This ambition releases any person to be free to live their life in any way they want to as long as their life exalts the majesty and greatness of God. That firm parameter will keep you from transgressing the line of right and wrong, and it will prevent evil from penetrating your "desire-to-glorify-God" force field.

Joseph fed the adulteress woman's intentions through that filter, and what came out the other side was an absolute and final answer: "How then can I do this great wickedness and sin against God?"

What Does This Mean?

When the guardian of your heart is the glory of the Lord, you're in a place to be a good friend, great lover, and beautiful spouse. This quality is the kind of person you want to marry. There are some ways you can discern if you're looking at a "whatever you do, do all to the glory of God" kind of person. I want to share with you three of those qualities.

Passionate – We are all passionate about something. To be passionate about the Lord is not something just for old Christians to emulate. Anybody can have a passion for God. If you're thinking about marrying someone, they should have a passion for God.

- Does he (or she) have a Godward orientation?
- Is the Lord what defines him?

At least one thing defines all of us. Nobody lacks passion. If you look long enough, you will find the something that makes your dating partner emote. If it is not the Lord, buyer beware. A desire to have a great job or to purchase a home or to build a future together are reasonable and necessary things. But when it comes to the Lord, a preeminent longing for His glory should make all other loves look like hate by comparison (Luke 14:26–27).

Repentable – Nobody has been able to pull off perfection but Jesus. This truth about fallenness means you will marry a sinner who will hurt your feelings. Joseph said, "How can I sin against God." The fact is that your spouse will sin against both you and God. I speak from experience as one who has sinned many times against my wife and my Lord.

Glorifying God does not imply perfection. Living a perfect life is contrary to the Bible—for all have sinned (Romans 3:23), and if any of us say we don't sin, we're liars (1 John 1:7–10). But do not fear. A person whose primary goal is to glorify God has a great backup plan: he will be a repenting person. Though he will have lapses in judgment, as experienced by doing something unkind to you, he will respond quickly with a broken-hearted confession (Psalm 51:17) plus a request for forgiveness. Why? His chief aim is to glorify God.

Community – A God-impassioned, repenting person will seek similar associations. Let me state it another way: regardless of who you are, you will find your kind. The question then becomes, "What kind of people are you seeking?" The Lord wired us with a herd mentality. It is not okay for us to be alone (Genesis 2:18), which is why we pursue community. If you're a loner, that community may be your video games or Internet surfing. You're no different from me in that you want to surround yourself with what you like (1 Corinthians 15:33).

You can take the measure of a person by assessing their associations—the things they fill their lives with so that they can enjoy life the way they want to. Nobody surrounds themselves with things they do not like. Even if they work a job they hate, they create hobbies to offset their disdain for their jobs.

We long for a community because God made us in the image of the original community (Genesis 1:26–27). How can the thing made be different from the person who made him? There is one way. It is a sin. The effect of sin is the only way we can have distorted desires for the wrong kind of community.

Presence, But Not Perfection

These three qualities will give you an indication of a person's desire to make God's name great in your relationship. But you want to be careful by making a distinction between the presence of these ideas and the perfection of them. Nobody will be able to glorify God perfectly. We are in a continuous sanctifying process. What you want to discern is the presence of these qualities, even if they are in early forms.

- Passion for God
- Repenting lifestyle
- Desire for community

If you have found the evidence of these things in your dating partner, you're at a great beginning. It is wise to ask other individuals who are familiar with both of you for their assessments of you. If you are unsure of the evidence you perceive in the person you want to marry, I appeal to you to not go forward (Romans 14:23). There should be nothing more important to you than a person's desire to glorify God. Do not let any other piece of information supplant that one, even if he assures you of his love for you. If you dismiss this advice, you will live to regret it.

Call to Action

1. Passion – What is your number one passion: the Lord's fame or something else? When there is nothing else for you two to talk about, what do you talk about: the Lord or something else?

2. Repentance – What does repentance look like in your relationship? How long does it take you both to confess your sins and forgive each other?

3. Community – Describe your community experience, the things that have a gravitational tug on your hearts. When you get to pick and choose what you want to do, what do you prefer? Who are the people and what are the things that have become your first companions?

Chapter 4

Best Reason

Biff and Mable are in love. When they came to their first premarital counseling session, I asked them why they wanted to get married. Mable explained how Biff finished her thoughts. I privately wondered how she would feel five years into the marriage after he stopped talking.

Then Mable said that he made her feel special. I wondered how she would feel after he became preoccupied with other things like his job. Mable added that he was handsome and how she could not believe someone as attractive as Biff wanted to marry her. I wondered how she would feel after old age crept up on both of them.

When it was Biff's turn, he said that he liked the idea of companionship because he did not enjoy being alone. I wondered how he would feel after she started nagging him about his habits. He said, somewhat sheepishly, that he could not wait to have sex. Both of them had kept themselves pure, waiting for their special day. I wondered how he would feel after the babies came and Mable would be too tired and overwhelmed for romance.

Biff and Mable's reasons for marriage were not bad ones. I am sure that most of us had similar thoughts when it was our time to tie the knot. They were serious about the Lord, and they desired to honor Him in everything. It was easy for me to relate to Biff's desire for companionship. God said it was not good for the man to be alone, and I do not like loneliness either. God created us for community life (Genesis 2:18).

The Father, Son, and Spirit—the first community—made us in their image. It seems that common sense would motivate the Lord to create humans to be like them, so He gave Adam a woman. It was good for Biff to desire a wife for himself. I was also glad that Biff was willing to state the obvious: he wanted to get married to be intimate with Mable. There is no reason for him to pretend his sexual drive was not real. It is a healthy desire for people who are called to marry. I respected his honesty.

And I liked Mable's desire for a complementarian relationship: she wanted someone to complete her, to finish her sentences. The Lord made Eve to supplement her husband and vice-versa.

Not the Best

Though their desires for each other were not wrong, there were a few things about them that caused concern. While they had good reasons for marriage, their ideas were not the best. I hoped to help them see a few things:

- All of their reasons were secondary reasons for marriage.
- All of them were preferences. They were desires, not needs.
- All of them would more than likely change at some point in their marriage.

Marriage is a permanent, lifetime, unbreakable relationship. The only thing that should break the marriage bond is death. That is why it is important for your primary reason for marriage to be the best one. Having a secondary purpose as the primary reason for marriage could be the death knell to the relationship. The strength of any marriage is tied directly to the reason for the marriage. If the reason goes away, you weaken the relationship.

That is why I privately wondered what would happen when Biff stops talking, does not make Mable feel special, or becomes less handsome. What if Mable begins to nag him or if she wants sex less? Their reasons for marriage must be stronger than the ones they gave. If not, they will be heading into rough waters without a sound understanding of marriage. They would become the majority report by joining that ever-growing number of unsatisfied married couples.

Strong, maturing, and joy-filled marriages are becoming rare in our Christian culture. No marriage is immune from trouble. In most of the marriage counseling that I have done, there were two common themes.

- They came to counseling within the first five years of their marriage.
- They came to counseling after fifteen or more years of marriage.

I rarely counsel couples between the five and fifteen-year mark. The reason most of my marriage counseling falls within those two groups is that the first five years are typically before the children come, or they are just on the cusp of parenting.

From the fifteen-year mark (and forward), the marriage embarks on the emptying nest period, when the children become more independent (self-reliant) as they prepare to move out of the home. If the young married couple does not access the help they need or make the appropriate adjustments to their marriage before the children come, two things will probably happen:

- He will be tempted to escape the marriage through his job.
- She will be tempted to escape the marriage through her children.

They will become two dissatisfied, disgruntled, and disconnected people who decided to reorient their marriage around their preferred distractions. Though this would not give them a God-centered marriage, they could survive the relationship with their distractions—at least until the kids leave home. At that point, it leaves the couple with nothing to distract them from themselves.

It is not unusual to hear about a couple getting a divorce after twenty-five or thirty years of marriage. Some people are shocked by this news. I am not. They ignored their problems and each other for as long as they could. After two decades of muddling along, there were no more distractions to keep them together, and the things they never corrected in the early years came back in force during the later years. The disappointments that passed under the bridge seemed nonreconcilable. They decide to part ways.

The Best

It is imperative that every young couple knows how and determines to build their marriage on the right foundation. It is nonnegotiable for a relationship that not only wants to go the distance but to go the distance with joy. Before I married Lucia, we began hammering out a marriage mission statement. We were aware of the statistics that pointed toward easy divorce. Nobody needs a good reason for divorce. If you do not like the person you married, all you need to do is play the irreconcilable differences card, and you can get a divorce without much effort.

We were also aware of the number of marriages around us that were not happy. I am not talking about non-Christian marriages but about the Christian ones. We knew many couples who were not exhibiting the love of Christ toward each other. We purposed not to get a divorce or resign ourselves to something less than God's best. That meant we had to build our marriage on something better than what we liked about each other.

- Companionship is great.
- Sex is fantastic.
- Finishing each other's thoughts is a perk.
- Being attractive is a plus, too.

None of those things should receive top billing in any marriage. We needed a better idea. This need is why we began to think about the implications of the gospel as it related to our union. We started to view our future marriage through a gospel lens.

Why Marry?

We went after the "why to marry" question by thinking about Christ—the gospel. Why did He come? Redemption. Christ came to redeem fallen man to Himself. We concluded there had to be a redemptive element to our marriage. In Ephesians 5:25–28, Paul gave all marriage partners a picture of the Lord's work by appealing to us to model the gospel in our covenant union. Marriage should be a redemptive image.

"Husbands, love your wives, as Christ loved the church and gave himself up for her, that he might sanctify her, having cleansed her by the washing of water with the word, so that he might present the church to himself in splendor, without spot or wrinkle or any such thing, that she might be holy and without blemish. In the same way, husbands should love their wives as their own bodies. He who loves his wife loves himself" (Ephesians 5:25–28).

Lucia and I began to think about our marriage as a picture of the gospel. We concluded that we could best glorify God by marrying each other so we could project, amplify, or magnify the image of Christ and the church more clearly to ourselves and others. We were not thinking about getting married just to be married. Thus, we wrote the following marriage mission statement.

We want to become one flesh because it will allow us to reflect Christ more effectively than by being single. Therefore, we pray our marriage will:

- *Manifest the relationship of Christ and His church to God.*
- *Manifest the relationship of Christ and His church to each other.*
- *Manifest the relationship of Christ and His church to our families and friends.*
- *Manifest the relationship of Christ and His church to the world.*

We pray our relationship will be (1) a sweet offering to God, (2) a blessing to each other, (3) a testimony to our families and friends, and (4) an opportunity to model Christianity to the world that is without hope.

As you can see from our marriage mission statement, we crafted a plan to put the beauty of Christ and His church on display. According to Paul, I am a picture of Christ, and Lucia is an image of the church. We both have the high privilege and joyful opportunity to make God's name great through our identification with Him.

Then It Went Wrong

We became one flesh and quickly did what I privately wondered if Biff and Mable would do. Even with an excellent plan, our marriage began to crumble. We drifted apart. We failed many times at trying to portray the gospel in our relationship. It was more than just my being a jerk, my hair

52

falling out, or my belly protruding farther than it used to. We slowly changed from the people who we were when we married.

There were three miscarriages. There were job losses. We gained new friends. We lost friends. We changed churches and changed homes. We had lots of money. We had no money. I cannot begin to count how many times I sinned against my wife. It would be safe to say that I sinned against her more than I have sinned against any other person in the world. We have had many desires throughout our marriage. She has had some for me. I have had some for her. We have had some for our life together. Some of them came to fruition, while others fell flat.

Through it all, and even in our darkest hours, there has been one constant: our main reason for getting married never changed. In all of our imperfections, we did want to reflect the gospel in our marriage. We work hard at this. Our world is dying, and we have an incredible opportunity to show them something that cannot be obtained but by Christ alone. Our true heart's desire is not to obscure the picture of Jesus and His church.

Why Reconcile?

Let me speak ever-so-briefly to how to respond when your relationship goes wrong. Perhaps your marriage mission statement is focused on changeable things rather than the unchangeable gospel. Maybe you are not living with the person you married. The things you liked about your spouse seem lost forever. Your spouse has evolved into another kind of person.

Maybe you need to reconcile with your marriage partner. Perhaps you are married, but you are muddling along. Maybe you have a low-grade disappointment as you reflect on how things were versus how things are.

• May I appeal to you to begin talking about a marriage redo?

- May I appeal to you to get some help?

You do not have to get a divorce. You do not have to continue down the same old grinding path. You can redefine your marriage, even if you are several years down that road. God is cool with a redo. You can start over no matter how far along you are.

- Will you do this?
- Will you seek help?

As you are waiting for help, you can begin to think about what you want your marriage to be. Let the gospel be what defines your marriage. You both are a picture of Christ and His church. Begin talking about how to present that picture:

- As an offering to the Lord,
- A blessing to each other,
- A testimony to family and friends, and
- An opportunity for the world to find hope through Christ.

The first step in this journey back to the gospel will be some long and challenging conversations. It is the only way that it will work. With your mind fixed on the gospel, which is the "process and the goal," begin praying about how to start talking to each other. Invite others into those discussions.

Call to Action

1. If you are thinking about marriage, take the content of this chapter and start writing out your marriage mission statement.
2. If you are married but need to make some changes in your marriage, I appeal to you to begin doing the same thing. Ask the Father to give you a glorious redo. He's cool with that.

Chapter 5

Warning Women

While it is true that people change as an ordinary course of aging, there is also another angle to this problem of being different in the future that I want to interact with here: dating couples lack careful assessment and outside input about getting married. Without sound biblical advice, love blinds, and if it does, there is a good chance that the couple will be set up for a lifetime of disappointment.

As you read this chapter, my appeal is for you to ask the Spirit of God to illuminate your mind and remove anything that hinders you from benefiting from the content of this chapter. Be open. Be honest. Be humble.

Try to read what I'm saying without the conflicting distractions of your desires or experiences. Momentarily die to yourself. Read as though this chapter was not about you. I'm asking you to think in the most biblically objective way you can. Perhaps it would be helpful if you read as though you were thinking about a friend.

What if you pretend that you are going to give "counsel" to your friend? What would you tell her after reading this chapter? I'm going to share with you some of the leading causes of marriage problems that have their roots in the dating relationship. I'm not dealing with every possible angle of the dating relationship, but I do want to highlight four major red flags that should cause a pause in any girl's heart regarding her boyfriend.

- Sexual Activity before Marriage
- Stealing the Heart of the Girl
- What You Should Like about Him
- Become a Good Sovereigntist

Sexual Activity before Marriage

Most of my marital counseling has been with couples who had consensual sex before they were married. And though their premarriage fornication does not represent all of their problems, you typically see a constellation of sinful patterns associated with their infidelity. I will talk about this problem in chapter ten. Here is a snippet:

Fornication is usually mishandled and, thus, not resolved. They may mask the problem but never, indeed, ignore it. If there is not biblical repentance, the long-term, residual effects that arise from premarital sex are impossible to overcome. Sin is real, and you must deal with it in biblical ways. If you have fornicated, you have to choose if you're going to confront this sin directly. Do not try to use denials, justifications, or rationalizations. You cannot fool sin.

Sin will extract payment from someone. It must. It's an unalterable law: sin requires a payment, which is the triumph and glory of Christ's death on the cross. Jesus paid for your sins, and you may repent and accept the payment that He made by His death on the cross.

If you have fooled around with your guy during the dating season, you are guilty before God, regardless of whether or not you went all the way. Let's not play games here. Don't try to deceive yourself by rounding the corners of your sin by saying,

"We didn't go all the way." That's deception. You know this. I know this. If you have sinned, I appeal to you to own it. Bring it to the light.

Though there are many things to say about sex before marriage, my main point is that if a man is willing to touch you, fondle you, rub you, or have sex with you, he lacks good sense and self-control. He is weak mentally, emotionally, and lacks biblical integrity and maturity. The Bible would call him a fool. It would benefit you to find every reference in the book of Proverbs about a fool, foolish, foolishness, or folly.

Do not think your boyfriend will all of a sudden grow up after you marry him. If he is willing to crawl across the Word of God to get his lust-filled hands on you, do you believe he will show more self-control and less selfishness after he ties the knot? If he is willing to defraud you and sin against God while he is on his best dating behavior, how do you think he is going to behave when he begins to presume on the relationship during your marriage? His current weaknesses will play out in many other areas of your future lives.

It is right and wise to assess him. Ask God to give you the clarity to observe other contexts where he is not behaving maturely. If you don't work through this now, within five years of your marriage, you will not respect him, and you will more than likely feel trapped.

- Has he touched you in any way that is inappropriate? If so, why did it happen? If so, why do you think he did it?
- What is wrong with his character if he is willing to defraud you this way?
- In what other ways do you see selfishness play out in his life?
- Will you let your parents, pastors, or primary authority caregivers know what happened?

Stealing the Heart of the Girl

It is not that difficult to take a young lady's heart. It is easier today than ever before. Girls are prewired by God to be captured and whisked away to an enchanted place by their knights in shining armor. All they need is a knight and, for some girls, any knight will do.

In today's culture, because of the dysfunction of the parental/ male role model, many girls are not only wired and ready to go, but they are angrily wired and are counting the days until they can do life on their terms, in their way, and with whomever they desire. They can't wait to carve out a better life with a better male, a better man than their previous experience with their fathers.

Insecure guys will dangle the marriage bait before the girl, and if she is vulnerable, angry, or desperate, she will probably take it. The immature man will do this instead of talking to her dad, pastor, or some other male authority in the girl's life. His first order of business is to get the girl rather than ask the parent for the girl.

Heart stealing is an unwise, immature, secretive agenda that can have a long-term, negative impact on your future marriage. This method of getting the girl is hard to repair. Typically, a wrong-footed beginning is how the relationship will continue unless God's grace intervenes. Without biblical repentance, a bad start will make for a challenging future. If you allow him to persist in this type of pre-conquest ritual of sensual advances and marriage talk without proper accountability and counsel, you may be well on your way to giving in and eventually becoming disillusioned.

• Was your heart stolen away or given away?
• Are you currently allowing him to take your heart?

- Who is carefully and wisely walking you through these things?
- Do you believe you are subjective in evaluating this relationship?
- What authority structures do you have in your life to help you think clearly?
- Are you aware of how the decisions you are making today will impact the rest of your life?

What You Should Like about Him

At some point, someone will ask you what you like about him. What will you say? Is it his personality, looks, work ethic, or how he treats you? While these things are not bad things, they are not the best things. As he ages, his personality will drastically change. His looks will decline. His physical ability and the economy will have a lot to do with his work ethic. How he treats you will also change in the coming years.

As your future husband changes, there must be one thing that changes for the better. If he loves the Lord God with all his heart, soul, mind, and strength, then his personality, looks, work ethic, and how he treats you will find submission to this transcending quality.

You must have full assurance that God is the point of your relationship rather than your boyfriend. Observe his life. Who is leading? You will know your answer by how he navigates your relationship. If your boyfriend is humble, submitted, and passionately following the leadership of Sovereign God, you are probably in a good place.

- How is he doing in loving God with his whole heart, mind, soul, and strength?

- How submitted is he to your parents, his parents, and his church?
- How active is he in the local church?
- How often does he confess his sins to you and others?
- What is his working knowledge and application ability of the Bible?
- Is he ready to be a father nine months from now?

This last question is an important one. If you were married today, it is possible you could be parents in nine months. Do you believe he is mature enough to hold down a job, take care of you, run a home, and father a child at this point in his life?

Become a Good Sovereigntist

- Has God told you to marry this person? How do you know?
- Why does God want you to marry this person?
- Why do you want to marry this person?
- What is your point and purpose in marrying this person?
- Are you in faith? Meaning, do you believe this is God's will for your life?
- Why did you answer that way?

If your boyfriend became a paraplegic tomorrow and was wheelchair-bound for the rest of his life, would you still believe you are to marry him? Do you have any doubt? If you answered "yes" or gave affirmative answers to this section of questions, what if you broke up and waited another year before you married him? If you are assured God wants you to marry this person— even if he became a paraplegic tomorrow, why don't you wait a year to see if he is the right guy for you?

I'm not asking you to do this. I'm challenging you to think deeply about one of the most important decisions you'll ever make. If God wants you to marry this person, no power on earth can stop you from marrying him. You will marry him, whether it is tomorrow, a year from now, or five years from now. Why do you have to marry him now? Be honest with your answer. Again, I'm not saying don't marry him now. I'm merely challenging your faith in moving forward.

"For whatever does not proceed from faith is sin" (Romans 14:23).

Do you doubt about marrying this person? If you have any doubts about any of the questions that I have asked you thus far or if anything in this chapter has caused you to pause, I appeal to you to put the relationship and possible marriage on hold. Walk away from it. Seek counsel. Make sure your heart is right before God. Remember, if God wants you to marry this guy, you will marry him. So, why sweat it? Take a break.

Regain clarity—especially if you both have been sexually inappropriate. Clear your heads and cool your jets. God is good, and He will take care of you, but if you persist in your way, He may let you choose a path to future disappointment.

Call to Action

1. I have asked you over thirty questions in this chapter. Will you go back and highlight and answer them over the next few weeks? As you do, will you talk to someone whom you respect and trust and who has the biblical wisdom, grace, and courage to not only assess your answers but biblically confront you in love—if you need confrontation?

2. If your dad is available, will you talk to him? A few weeks of biblical reflection is a small price to pay when the rest of your life is at stake.

Chapter 6

For the Man

Girls are unique individuals that every dad, husband, and boyfriend need to understand. Regardless of their age, there are universal truths that apply to all girls. Did you know that girls have a "call to submission" that is different from a man's call to submit? What are some of the things that you, as a future husband, could do to make it easier for your future wife to submit with joy?

You will find the answers to my questions in a proper understanding of how women are different from men. Those differences, and the male's role in understanding and practically living out those differences, are the topic of this chapter.

Submitting to Submission

All women who choose to marry will interact with three primary authority figures in their lives:

- She must submit to God.
- She must submit to her father.
- If she marries, she must submit to her husband.

Within the marriage and family constructs, there are biblical hierarchies that God commands us to follow. These hierarchies have nothing to do with being loved more or less by God, but they do have a lot to do with living in an ordered way in God's world while representing Him effectively to others. We submit to governments, employers, and church authorities. Children submit to their parents, and wives submit to their husbands. It is a reasonable, understandable, and biblical idea, but submission is only one side of the relationship.

The other "side of submission" expects and demands responsibility upon all those who are in authority to lead well. Fathers are not to provoke their children (Ephesians 6:4). Employers should direct their employees in a God-glorifying way (1 Peter 2:18–20). Husbands have a biblical responsibility to motivate their wives to submit (Ephesians 5:25–33; 1 Peter 3:7).

The Father's Picture

A little girl's daddy is her first and primary authority figure that calls for her submission. He is the one who will set the stage for how she will eventually view God as Father and submit to Him. This responsibility is why dads are called to model God (Philippians 4:9). They are to imitate God (Ephesians 5:1). And all dads are to follow God (1 Corinthians 11:1) as they put Him on display (Galatians 2:20). Biblical fathers teach their children about God (Deuteronomy 6:4-9) and lead them to God (Proverbs 22:6).

All daughters will learn—to some degree—how to think about, understand, and respond to God the Father through the strongest and earliest picture that they will ever see, which is their fathers. The most radical instance that I saw of this was a lady whom I was counseling many years ago, who began to cry during our counseling session spontaneously.

I asked, "Why are you crying?"

She said, "I am crying because I was looking at your Bible."

I asked, "Why are you doing that?"

She said, "When I look at your Bible, it reminds me of God the Father. When I think about God the Father, it reminds me of my father. When I think about my dad, I cry. He was a cruel man."

Though her case was darker than most children, as far as the cruelty of a father goes, the idea of a "heavenly Father to earthly father" connection is not an exception when it comes to how girls typically build their filter for viewing God the Father. Any father could potentially corrupt a girl's understanding of a father. Here are the three most common ways:

- He can die.
- He can divorce his wife.
- He can be in the home but not model a clear picture of God the Father.

It is not unusual for a girl to come to Christ and then have to begin a process of learning who God the Father is because she was given a corrupted picture, as portrayed by her dad.

Keep Your Picture Clear

Years ago I told my children that I am a picture of God the Father. I said that to them because I already knew that what they were seeing in me was being connected to the idea of a father. After a long pause I followed up with this one major caveat: I sin, and God will never sin. My ability to sin, especially against them and their mother, is probably the most striking difference between me and God the Father. That is why it is stupendously vital for me to repent to my wife and children when I sin against them (or in their presence).

If I do not remove my sin by nailing it to the cross of Christ (1 John 1:7–9; Colossians 2:14), they will more than likely become confused as to what a good father should be. Here are two typical examples of what can confuse children by blurring the image of God the Father.

- If I love them conditionally (Ephesians 2:9). Meaning, if I love them only when they are meeting my expectations, I will incite their Adamic desires to perform to win my affection (Proverbs 29:25).
- If I criticize them more than I encourage them (Ephesians 4:29), I will further incite those desires because they will feel as though they can never fully measure up to my standards (2 Corinthians 10:12).

Without carefully walking them through my sins and sin patterns, you can rest assured that should they "come to God" through regeneration (John 3:7), they will carry "my effect" on them into their relationship with God (Ephesians 4:22). If I am not repenting to God and my children, they will have a corrupted view of a good father. In time, after they become teenagers, they will discern the actual truth about me, and if the grace of God does not intervene at that point, they may choose to walk away from God and me because of their anger and distrust in both of us.

- What kind of picture of God the Father has your girlfriend's dad portrayed to her?
- If she is amenable to you both discussing these things, will you speak to her about what you have read here?

New Day – New Man

If a dad has done his job reasonably well and has been repenting all along the way when he has failed, he should be able to give a mature, biblically sound, and submitting daughter to her new husband. The little girl will leave her dad and mom and

66

cleave to her husband (Genesis 2:24–25). If the man knows how to continue to serve his new wife the way her daddy did, it can be a near flawless transition that should set them up for a beautiful marriage.

The Other Side of the Coin – If her new husband has not received sound shepherding, in a similar godly way as his wife, he will not be able to satisfactorily fulfill his role as a spouse—at least not in the beginning. Until he "gets up to speed" on how to love his wife the way Christ loved the church (Ephesians 5:25), she will have to learn how to enjoy God in spite of his shortcomings.

His husbandry skills will be like a birthmark on someone's face. In one sense, it does not hinder anything, but in another sense, you'll always know it's there. In the case of his wife, she can adjust to her marriage disappointment because God provides grace for such disappointments (1 Corinthians 10:13).

Back to the Garden

The problem with this type of marriage is that the husband has not learned and applied biblical submission to his life. There are two sides to submission, which requires equal responsibility, humility, and maturity. Because of the unique authority/submission relationship in a marriage, it is essential for both the dad and the husband to understand their roles in creating a grace-filled environment that motivates the females in their lives to submit.

The call to submission should not be any stronger than the call to lead well by providing a grace-filled, joy-filled, and love-filled environment that motivates the person to submit.

Submission is the call on all our lives. Thus far, I have been speaking mostly about the female's role in submission. But the male is also called to submit to a higher authority. We see this in the first individuals whom God created. In the beginning, the male was Adam, and the higher authority was God. The Father created Adam, and Adam submitted to Him. Then the Father created Eve, and she submitted to Adam. This "creation submission construct" set the hierarchy for relationships.

The Father provided Adam with a loving and safe environment for him to flourish in. And it was Adam's job to do for his wife what the Lord was doing for him—to provide a loving and safe environment for her to flourish in. Though God did many other things for Adam, I think you will find that all of those things were within these two parameters: (1) His great love for Adam and (2) His protective care of Adam. Those are the two primary things that all of us need to flourish well in God's world.

- Will I be loved well by God?
- Will I be safe if I follow Him?

It was the removal of God's love and protective care that sent Adam, Eve, and the whole world into chaos (Genesis 2:16–17; 3:6–19). This chaotic problem is what makes John 3:16 such a cherished Bible passage. In that one verse, we see God's great love—I will send my Son to die in your place—and His protective care—you are eternally secure with me.

"For God so loved the world, that he gave his only Son, that whoever believes in him should not perish but have eternal life" (John 3:16).

Giving What You Got

Adam and Eve were different, but the things they wanted were the same: (1) to be loved and (2) protected. While God made Adam and drew Adam to Himself, Eve came out of the man and was naturally drawn to him (Genesis 2:18–25). Now it was Adam's turn to do for Eve what God did for him: to love and protect his bride. He had a responsibility to image his Creator in a similar way in which he had experienced Him.

- How are you imaging the love of God to your girlfriend?
- How are you imaging the protective care of God to your girlfriend?

To be loved and to be protected are the two conditions that will motivate any girl to submit to the male authority figure in her life. If you do not believe this, I appeal to you to talk to your girlfriend about what I have written here. Ask her the importance of these two things from you to her. Your girlfriend is being asked to do something rather profound: to give up her individual life to blend into you and to follow you for the rest of your lives.

Submission is profound, and it is also what God is asking all of us to do: to die to ourselves to follow Him. What do you think biblical submission means? Submission is a sacrifice made by faith in someone (Romans 10:17) who will love and protect you well (Romans 8:31–39). It was the kindness (love) of God that led to your repentance (Romans 2:4), and you willingly fell in love with God because you believed that He would take care (protect) of you (John 3:16; Romans 8:37). You submitted to Him because there were two things that you knew.

- You would be profoundly loved.
- You would be eternally secure.

A Daddy's Love

A dad has an incredible and fantastic job description regarding his daughter. He has the privilege to model the love and protective care of God the Father to his daughter. She will submit by default to him while she is young. That is what children usually do.

She will not submit to her daddy as she becomes a teenager if he has not imaged the protective care and compelling love of God to her. If he does model God the Father well, there is a good chance she will not be tempted to satisfy her God-given desires for love through sinful means after she becomes a teenager.

Teen girls, who are crazy about boys, are almost always looking (1) to be loved by them and (2) to feel safe with them. The love they crave is lust, and the security they long for is to fill an insecure void their dads left because of their unwillingness to image God the Father to them. If the teen girl becomes desperate enough, she will latch on to any person. If she follows through by marrying that kind of person, she will probably regret her decision for the rest of her life.

A Husband's Love

In nearly every case when a wife commits adultery, it is motivated by her desire to be loved and protected by a man. Her craving for those things becomes so intense that the hideousness of adultery pales in her mind.

Friend, I wish I could open up your head and pour this chapter into your brain so that you could see the culpable role you play in pushing your future wife into the arms of another man. Too often with the adultery of a woman, the husband has been neglectful in loving and protecting her well. He became preoccupied with other things like his work. He became unkind (un-love) and harsh (un-safe) toward her. He did very little encouraging while growing more critical of her. While I would never condone a wife's adultery or a teen's lust for boys, it is essential to fully engage all the responsible parties that created such an outcome.

Call to Action

Let's Start with Dad

1. Dad, is your little girl profoundly aware of your affection for her?
2. Does she know that no matter what happens, she will always be protected, safe, and secure because of your undeniable love for her?
3. Is she more aware of your encouragement of her or your displeasure with her?
4. Are you daily repenting of the things that blur the image of God the Father to her?
5. How does she view God the Father? Do you know?
6. Are you aware of the theological filter that you gave her—the one in which she sees God the Father?

A Few Questions for the (Future) Husband

1. Does your wife experience daily cherishing and nourishing from you?
2. Are you aware of her secret thoughts that may be bringing division into your marriage?
3. Will you ask her to talk to you about how she feels and experiences your love for her?
4. Will you ask her to speak to you about how she feels and experiences your protective care?
5. Where does she rank on your list of priorities?
6. How are you helping her to keep from taking her desire for love and protection and turning it into a need that drives her to sin?

Chapter 7

A Man's Struggle

Sex is a beautiful thing, though a sinful sexual temptation is not. After the fall, every person has struggled with distorted views of sex and sexual temptation. In this chapter, I will be addressing every man's battle with sex, which I will begin by asking you a critical question: how do you think about those who are not free from sexual temptation?

When some people think about sexually tempted people, they immediately relegate them to the perverted regions of human depravity. That kind of thinking is myopic, unkind, and unhelpful. To cast every sexually tempted person under the bus of perversion is immature, ignorant, and arrogant (self-righteous). Sexual temptation is a universal temptation for men (and women) because it is supposed to be.

The Lord built into men a desire to like and enjoy the opposite sex. It would have been a major relational faux pas if the Lord created man without a desire for a woman. If God had placed naked Eve in front of naked Adam and Adam had not liked what he was looking at, that would have been weird. I suppose Adam could have thanked the Lord for giving him a helper and went out to play with the animals.

"And the rib that the Lord God had taken from the man he made into a woman and brought her to the man. Then the man said, 'This at last is bone of my bones and flesh of my flesh; she shall be called Woman, because she was taken out of Man.' Therefore a man shall leave his father and his mother and hold fast to his wife, and they shall become one flesh. And the man and his wife were both naked and were not ashamed" (Genesis 2:22–25).

But Adam did not go out and play with the animals. He wanted to play with his new playmate. You hear it in his voice: "At last," I have someone that I can connect with, a person with whom I can relate. Eve was different from the rest of God's creative work. And she was different from Adam, which made them perfect for each other. They fit like a hand in a glove. You sense this in the instinctive attraction that he had for her. She was different, and he desired her.

When some individuals talk about sexual temptation, they don't go back far enough. If they do go back at all, they only go back to Genesis 3 where man's view and practice of sex was distorted and depraved by sin. If you're going to talk about sex, the essential place to begin is how sex and sexual relationships were always supposed to be. Sex was good, and Adam and Eve enjoyed their sexual relationship. They were not ashamed but were naked and shared the most intimate love relationship that two humans can enjoy with each other.

Do you think Adam or Eve stopped liking sex after sin took over their lives? Did the way the Lord made them regarding their sexual drive stop after the fall? They did not experience a decreased sex drive or sexual desires because of their fall. They continued to enjoy sex and felt drawn to each other. What they were and what they liked before the fall continued to be part of their passions after the fall.

Take Food

The desire for sex is no different from any other good thing the Lord had made before hell broke loose on man's soul. Genesis 3 did not eradicate the good things the Lord made, though the fall did change how humanity thought about and desired those things. Imagine if the Lord made food and made man dependent on food but put a distaste for food on man's palate. That does not sound like a good God. He creates things perfectly, which means the food is not just for utilitarian purposes. God made food tasty so that man could enjoy it while he was storing his survival energy in his belly. He did this by giving man taste buds.

- Man desires food.
- Man eats food.
- Man enjoys food
- Man benefits from food.

It was a perfect plan. How kind of God to make things this way. Then sin entered the world. What changed? Nothing in the sense that man still desired, ate, enjoyed, and benefited from food. The fall did not create a different kind of man who had no connection to his pre-fallen condition.

Sin did not remove man's pre-fall enjoyment of and benefit from food, but it did distort how man thought about food. He could no longer have a perfect godly experience with food. No longer was he able to desire, eat, enjoy, and benefit from food. His newly depraved mind took good food and twisted it into a means to feed his selfish desire to indulge himself.

He no longer ate food for God's glory alone (1 Corinthians 10:31). Adam and Eve's God-centered worldview turned into a dark man-centered one. If there is a way to distort the Lord's kindnesses to us, we will find that way. We have the depraved ability to turn all God's blessings into personal indulgence. Food is good and meant for all to enjoy, but we are tempted to make poor food choices as well as eating more than we should.

Twisted Sex

Our sex problems, like food or any gift from the Lord, are one of our most complicated, distorted blessings from God. To reprimand a person for desiring sex does not help him untangle sin's distortions. To call a person evil because they make poor food choices or overeat is as wrongheaded. You don't help a person change through corrupting speech (Ephesians 4:29).

To condemn a person each time of temptation is like asking him not to be human. Rather than convicting him, it would be better to understand how his twisted heart became that way due to fallenness. Your temptation may be different, but the truths to remember are that you do experience temptations and that you have not fully conquered all of them.

I am not condoning sexual sin. I'm appealing for a more intelligent discussion about God's design and our desire for sex, a desire that the fall did not eradicate. There are two extremes with some people regarding improper biblical discourse.

- The sexually tempted person will go to great lengths to justify their favorite kind of sinful sexual practice.
- The untempted individual will uncharitably jump on any person who struggles with sinful sexual temptation.

No one can condone sinful sex of any kind because God does not excuse immorality. There is no stamp to approve some form of immoral sex. And the only acceptable type of sex is the kind that happens between a man and a woman after they are married. Any other kind of sex places the participants under the judgment of God. Unbiblical sex is the practice of darkened and futile minds.

"Let marriage be held in honor among all, and let the marriage bed be undefiled, for God will judge the sexually immoral and adulterous" (Hebrews 13:4).

"They are darkened in their understanding, alienated from the life of God because of the ignorance that is in them, due to their hardness of heart. They have become callous and have given themselves up to sensuality, greedy to practice every kind of impurity" (Ephesians 4:18–19).

Post-Genesis-3 Struggler

There is a difference between a person who is making excuses for their gluttony and the person who is honest about their temptation to overeat. If a person comes to you and says they are tempted to graze, overeat, or find comfort in food, I recommend that you do not condemn them but rather thank them. If they have the humility and trust to let you know they are a Genesis 2 person who has been twisted by Genesis 3, encourage them to continue in dialogue as you keep watch on your heart since you're a struggler, too (Galatians 6:1–2; Matthew 18:33).

Don't brand them like a pervert or a lesser person in the human race because they are honest about how God made them and how the devil has twisted them. Their struggle may be because impure thoughts control them. Maybe they are overly tempted. It could be because something happened to them in their childhood that twisted their understanding of sex and its purposes. I do not know why they may have a twisted perspective and practice of sex, but I do want to make sure they know these two things.

- They are experiencing something reasonable, which is why I want to sympathize with them (Hebrews 4:15).
- I want to applaud their desire for the opposite sex. That is a good thing, designed by God.

To not struggle (Romans 3:10–12) or not desire the opposite sex denies the truth of God's Word. Unfortunately, the sexually tempted person has a heart like mine and yours. We all have our dark battles with sin's temptations. The sexually tempted mind does not understand a gospel orientation for sex. Rather than seeing sex as for the other person, they have turned sex onto themselves. The gospel orientation for sex has the receiver in view because the gospel is always object focused (John 3:16).

The Lord gave all His gifts so that others could benefit from them. Sadly, we live in a post-Genesis-3 world, which means our temptation is to take God's blessings and turn them onto ourselves to feed and satisfy our selfish pleasures. Rather than seeing sex as a gift to give to his spouse, the sexually tempted person sees himself as the receiver of sexual pleasure. A gospel orientation makes others the receiver of the blessing; a selfish orientation makes yourself the receiver of the benefit.

Call to Action

The Parent

Sexual temptation will be part of your child's life. He may be cute, cuddly, and oblivious right now, but he will not always be that way. Be warned and be discerning about how God made him to enjoy sex and be proactive as you think about how his fallenness will try to distort sex. Your worst move is to bury your head in the sand by thinking your child is different. No child is different when it comes to any version of distorted sex. There is no select group of untempted men—no matter how godly they are or how devout you want to think they are.

"He raised up David to be their king, of whom he testified and said, 'I have found in David the son of Jesse a man after my heart, who will do all my will'" (Acts 13:22).

"It happened, late one afternoon, when David arose from his couch and was walking on the roof of the king's house, that he saw from the roof a woman bathing; and the woman was very beautiful" (2 Samuel 11:2).

The Wife

Your husband (or boyfriend) is not an anomaly. It is wise and humble for husbands and wives to talk about these things. The gospel should have freed you by this time (Hebrews 5:12–14). It should have you in such a place where there is nothing to hide and nothing to protect. If you're unwilling to talk about your sanctification journey, specifically about this crucial aspect of that journey, I would recommend that you find help because your marriage is not as healthy as it should be.

The Tempted

"But each person is tempted when he is lured and enticed by his own desire. Then desire when it has conceived gives birth to sin, and sin when it is fully grown brings forth death" (James 1:14–15).

Friend, you are tempted toward the wrong kind of sex, but do not be discouraged: temptation and yielding to temptation are two remarkably different things, though there is only a thin line that separates them. To tempt is an essential play from the devil.

He knows every human has some attraction for the thing that he is swinging in front of their craving hearts (James 4:1–2). If a man were not prewired to like what the devil was tempting him with, the devil would not try to tempt him with it. He only lures you if you're willing to succumb to the temptation.

Something tempts every individual. Though the consequences of some sins can be more grievous than others, do not think your "non-sex sin" puts smaller nails in the hands of Christ (James 2:10). Only the person struggling with gospel amnesia would slam the door on a sexual struggler as though that person has a plague, which also includes the gay community. We all have our problems. Yours may put you in a more likable category within the Christian community but not before God: we're all filthy in His eyes (Isaiah 64:6) and stand in need of Christ's righteousness.

Call to Action

1. Can you admit that you struggle with temptation?
2. Do you see yourself as better than other people? If so, what good merit makes you better?
3. Do you treat strugglers the way that the Lord responds to you when you bring your struggles to Him?

"And should not you have had mercy on your fellow servant, as I had mercy on you?" (Matthew 18:33).

Chapter 8

A Man's Temptation

You marry all of your future husband, including his mind, which is why you want to give careful and courageous scrutiny to a few things that are easy to overlook in the name of love, as well as inherent inhibitions and insecurities. Dating, sexuality, and understanding temptation are essential discussions that a couple must delve into at some point if they are planning on marrying. Sin has tainted all aspects of your lives, and sex-related issues is one of the most significant ones.

A way to navigate this dating dilemma is by taking the plunge and finding out the answers to a few critical questions about your boyfriend's perspective and experience with sex and sensuality. Of course, it will depend on a few things like your collective spiritual maturities and biblical transparency. Each couple is different, so you'll need God's wisdom as you prepare to take your relationship to this critical level. Perhaps it would be wise to talk to a spiritual authority in your life as you move toward this necessary communication opportunity. Before you talk to your boyfriend, share this chapter with that mentor.

Let's assume that you will marry each other soon, that you're both mature in Christ, and that you've been growing in transparency. You have also gained the advice of your mentor. Here are a few suggestive but essential questions for you to consider asking your boyfriend as it pertains specifically to porn and masturbation. This list on sex and temptation is not exhaustive; you may want to add other questions or adapt these.

- Have you ever looked at porn? If yes, how much porn did you view?
- How often did you look at porn?
- What were some of the ways you used porn?
- Why did you do it?
- Who knew about it?
- Who did you seek for help?
- When was the last time you masturbated? If yes, why did you masturbate?
- How often have you masturbated this past year? The past five years?
- What accountability measures do you have in your life to help you work through sexual temptation?

Getting Personal with Your Boyfriend

These questions are personal questions, and I suppose they would make most people uncomfortable. I have dealt with these things for decades, nearly on a weekly basis. Sexual temptation is on a short list of the most common problems in which we all struggle. Putting my vocation aside for the moment, I do not see them as too personal as much as I see them as loving, self-protective questions.

If you're planning to marry someone, the more profound and more personal your questions should be for the person whom you love. The more bound you are to a person, the more you need scrutiny for your long-term well-being. Jesus may have been reluctant to get up in the Pharisees' business (John 2:24–25), but He was not timid or hesitant with those who were closest to Him (Matthew 16:23).

If a girl is thinking about committing the rest of her life with a guy, those questions are necessary. Which would be worse: to ask personal questions before your wedding day or to be devastated ten years into your marriage after you find out that he has a sexual addiction? With that said, I don't want you to think I'm dismissing any inherent tentativeness with these types of questions. There is a dark side to the adult world, and it should cause a cautious and wise posture in your soul. Many Christian women have not experienced exposure to some of the seedier things in our culture.

Thus, I appeal to you to ask the Spirit to give you the thought-filled illuminations and empowering grace that you will need as you launch into the longest and most challenging time of your life. And though I don't want to put your future marriage on par with buying a car, please allow me to use an illustration.

When purchasing a car, a wise person would not hold back from asking all the right questions. She researches, investigates, compares, and asks the hard things. Why? She is about to make a significant commitment. How much more wisdom and courage do you need when thinking about your marriage? It is common for many unions that go off the rails to miss out on these essential discussions while they were dating. They do not fully explore these talks because of their most common tendencies.

- Girls typically lead with romantic notions and utopian dreams.
- Guys tend to lead with hormonal desires.

Read between the Lines

As for the questions, if he has looked at porn, he more than likely has masturbated. It would be exceptional if that were not the case. If he has looked at porn and is honest with you about what he has done, go ahead and assume that he has masturbated. Don't bury your idealistic head in the sand. If he has sought help, you can ask him if you can talk to the person who helped him so that you can gain a third-party's perspective.

If your boyfriend is humble, open, and honest, he has nothing to hide and nothing to protect. A gospel-centered worldview compels a Christian to a higher opinion, which empowers him to fight the temptation to conceal his sins or protect his reputation. Free men are free. They are not habitually bound, insecure, or easily offended.

If he doesn't let you speak into his life at this level at this time, consider it a red flag. One of the most common complaints that I hear in marriage counseling is a husband's unwillingness to let his wife probe into his life. These husbands resist openness, honesty, and transparency. If you are planning to marry this guy, and if he opposes your questions, consider his response a precursor to what your future marriage experience would be like.

It would be fair to multiply his replies to you—whether good or bad—by ten after you are married. Our good or bad behaviors will only increase after marriage. Only repentance can change a sinful trajectory. Dating is the wonderful, charmed, fun, romantic, put-your-best-foot-forward—but a somewhat artificial —season, where you do not see the most accurate colors of each other. While you may have had arguments and disappointments during the dating season, whatever has happened will pale in comparison to a 24/7, uninterrupted bond, which will only break at death.

Signs and Attitudes

The first sign that you should look for is how he responds to your questions. That will tell you nearly all you need to know, though there are other things you will need to discern. For example, how close to the edge does he walk regarding sexual issues? Paul told us to flee youthful lusts (2 Timothy 2:22). Which direction does he lean: toward sexual passion or does he run from it?

"Keep your way far from her, and do not go near the door of her house" (Proverbs 5:8).

The language of Scripture is severe, strong, and clear when it comes to lust. You don't go there. If a person does, it will be perceived eventually. Here are a few things you can look for as far as signs and attitudes:

- What kind of language does he use? Does he use sexual language? Flirty language? Sexually tempting language? Sexually crude language?
- How does he treat you? How does he treat his mother? How does he treat his sisters, if he has any? You're trying to discern how he treats women, especially those who have been the closest to him. You will be the closest to him in marriage.
- Where does he touch you? Does he protect you and your body?
- Does he look at the opposite sex in ways that seem inappropriate? Do his eyes follow a lady as she walks into a room? Can he be easily distracted by the opposite sex?
- Does he have a problem watching R-rated movies, the ones that have sexual content in them? Does he think proactively when it comes to movies? Does he quickly look away when sexual images are in front of him?
- Does he talk to you about his temptations? Is he open about his weaknesses—in an appropriate way for communicating such things? Does he ask you to help him guard his heart—to pray for him? As you go deeper into the relationship, he

should be more honest with you. If not, you and your boyfriend will be easily tempted to fornicate.

- Is he modest with what he wears? Does he want you to dress modestly?

Which Is Worse?

Some girls have asked, "Is there a difference between struggling with lust—with seeing girls dressed immodestly or in the media—versus struggling with pornography?" The answer is "yes" and "no." There is an obvious difference, but the better question is, "What's the relationship between these two actions?" As you go through the section on signs and attitudes, you should be able to discern if looking at girls and media are the appetizers to the main event.

If he does not struggle with or if he responds in a mature way to the cultural temptations of immodesty, there is a good chance he does not struggle with pornography. My mother used to say, "Where there is smoke, there is fire." It applies here. If he struggles with the signs and attitudes, you may have a problem. The writer of Proverbs answered your question this way: "Can a man carry fire next to his chest and his clothes not be burned? Or can one walk on hot coals and his feet not be scorched?" (Proverbs 6:27–28).

While there are differences between cultural temptations and addiction to porn, the cultural temptations are often the precursor to more destructive sin patterns. The key that you're looking for with the addicted person is their attitude and response toward their sin. Let me illustrate this with the life of David, specifically his sexual sin with Bathsheba. We understand that David lived in unrepentant sin for at least a year before Nathan confronted him. (Bathsheba had already given birth to their son.) We also know that he was under deep conviction from the Lord. (See Psalm

32:1–4.) As you read Psalm 32, you realize the power of the Lord's conviction: David could not continue in an unrepentant state for long.

There is not a strong case in Scripture for the multi-year, backsliding Christian. The mantra often used by people who "got saved at five but walked away from the Lord, and now they are thirty-five" is problematic. One of the few testimonies we have of a person who walked away from the Lord in Scripture is David, and this is what he said about that season of his life: "For when I kept silent, my bones wasted away through my groaning all day long. For day and night your hand was heavy upon me; my strength was dried up as by the heat of summer" (Psalm 32:3–4).

I'm not sure how you can walk away from the Lord for thirty years and experience what he experienced. With that said, I think I can make an argument for a person who is caught in addiction and who can still be a Christian. I've seen it too many times not to believe this. I have counseled a few addicted people, and I do not think all of them were unbelievers. I'm talking about individuals with a multi-decade addiction. Paul's language in Galatians seems to support this.

"Brothers, if anyone is caught in any transgression, you who are spiritual should restore him in a spirit of gentleness" (Galatians 6:1).

The word caught is the Bible word for addiction. First Corinthians 6:9–11 is an excellent text about habitual sinning but not a solid one for this discussion. The general idea in Corinthians is the person who is a blatant rebel against God—a person who doesn't care about God—a reviler. Based on all the texts that speak to sinning Christians, I don't think you can make a case that a habitual sinner is automatically an unbeliever. There are many Christians who bring addictive lifestyles into their relationships with God (Ephesians 4:22), and sometimes it takes years for them to overcome.

The key you are looking for is their attitude about their sin. Are they humble, honest, open, transparent, and seeking help? Or are they hiding, defiant, and slandering the Word of God? The first group could be Christians while the latter group probably is not.

Call to Action

1. What have been your parents' observations about him?
2. If you have a sister, what are her thoughts about your boyfriend?
3. Consider asking your pastor (or another spiritual leader) their thoughts about him.
4. What has been his dating, sensual history? Is he a serial dater? Has he been a one-and-done guy?
5. What do you believe the Lord is guiding you to do now based on what you've read?

Chapter 9

Kissing Differently

God made Adam a unique male and Eve a unique female. I don't think this is news to anyone, especially to those who are married. And did you also know that a man is not affected by love in the same way a woman experiences love? The typical guy takes a more physical approach to love, while the ordinary girl takes a more emotional approach. It does not make either one of them wrong: they are just different.

When a boy meets a girl, it is more of a physical encounter than an emotional moment. It is easy and natural for his mind to move toward sexual arousal, while she may be more inclined to entertain romantical thoughts and expectations. This difference is why a boy kissing a girl can excite his hormones, which can tempt him to fast track to a more dynamic and steamier physical interplay. And though the act of kissing can just as easily lead to physical interaction with a girl, it is initially about emotional engagement, relational harmony, and a sense of belonging for her.

Though they both will feel these kinds of things, neither one of them would be able to articulate what's happening entirely. It is rare for a young couple to be that in tune to the intricate dynamics of relational desires and hormonal cravings. This lack of awareness is where candid conversations and biblical leadership are essential for the parents of a young person who is looking for love in a lasting relationship.

- Dad and mom, how are you doing at walking your child through the realities of dating, kissing, touching, and sex?
- How are you preparing your children by helping them to guard their hearts?

If the Shoe Fits

Most girls want to be married, and they want their guy to romance them. They come prewired by God to be pursued, to be looked at, and to be loved (Genesis 2:22–23). There is a reason Prince Charming has become a metaphor for the pursuer, and Cinderella hopes and prays the shoe will fit her foot. A girl should not feel odd or different because she desires to be loved by a guy. It is a biblical idea. If she were wired to react repulsively at the thought of a man, marriage would be a problem and procreation would never happen. Perhaps when she was a little girl, she said something like, "Boys? Yuck!"

That day has passed. She is not your little girl any longer. God made her long for companionship. It is our job as parents to be intentional by predetermining that we will serve our girls in the area of guarding their hearts. The unguarded heart is one of the biggest dangers of dating. Most young people will not have the discernment needed to keep themselves from crossing the line with the opposite sex. It's analogous to giving a ten-year-old the keys to the car. Don't expect them to get it right. And a young twenty-something could never fully understand the depths and contours of love and the accompanying temptations that come with it.

I have counseled scores of forty-year-olds who still have not figured out what love is all about—the giving and receiving of mature love. The apostle Paul appealed to us to refrain from hastily or unwittingly encouraging or expecting our girls to enter into relationships where they unleash inner longings too early.

"So flee youthful passions and pursue righteousness, faith, love, and peace, along with those who call on the Lord from a pure heart" (2 Timothy 2:22).

He told Timothy to flee youthful lusts and to pursue righteousness, faith, love, and peace—all with a pure heart. Dad, it's not just about talking to your daughter about what she ought not to be doing. It is also about giving her a vision regarding what she needs to be doing (Ephesians 4:22–24).

- Do you think a dating relationship helps them to flee youthful lusts while enabling them to pursue righteousness, faith, love, and peace from a pure heart?
- How are you protecting her from the trap of love?

The preceding two questions are not suggesting that dating is wrong. Whether it's right for a girl to date is not the issue. Discernment regarding the best situation for your daughter is what is at stake, as you factor in the kind of person she is and the kind of person that is best for her.

Sex Is a Leadership Issue

Guys, you have a huge responsibility when you enter into a relationship with a girl. If she likes you, she will have a hard time resisting you. If you cross the line with her, she will more than likely follow you. God made her so that she would fall in love with you. This willingness to be vulnerable is not a weakness on her part but a means that leads to something beautiful. But that "beauty" is rendered ugly if either partner is irresponsible, which is why dating is a leadership issue for you.

- How are you going to lead her? Will it be to satisfy your hormonal cravings or to put Christ and His church on display by your relationship?
- Are you leading her toward righteousness, faith, love, and peace?

Dating is also a stewardship issue. Your leadership in and stewardship of the dating relationship will have a significant impact on how it goes now and how things will be in the future.

The boyfriend may ask, "Is she responsible if she follows my poor leadership?" Of course, she is. She is entirely guilty if she does not pump the brakes on a relationship that is heading toward biblical boundary crossing. You cannot diminish her guilt and participation in a relationship that has gone too far, as though she is an innocent victim. But for now, the main issue is to zero in on the role of the guy who is called to be the biblical leader in romantic relationships. If a man crawls over the Word of God to satisfy his lust-filled cravings, you are getting a peek into his leadership style, his abilities, and his objectives in the relationship. Let the preceding statement be your warning.

He is showing you his character as he is leading you, regardless of how he is leading you. Though you may feel "lost in the moment" of your love desires and you believe that your hidden heart cravings may feel satisfied, if you do not make a course correction, you will be set up for years of marital heartache. Parents, did you think about this when you were dating? The majority of us did not. Typically, premarital sex and how it distorts relationships does not cross the mind of a young adult. Most young people do not care.

I could not fully understand the complexity of fornication—premarital sex—before I became a forty-something-year-old man. It was after I began helping people untangle their miserable marriages that the impact of sex during the dating years became more evident to me. Most of the unhappy marriages I have counseled began the very way that I'm warning you about now. They were just harmlessly dating, having fun, enjoying foreplay, and maybe having intercourse. They say, "Everybody is doing it. What's the problem, you old-stick-in-the-mud?"

You Had Me at Hello

The problem is that sex is a leadership and stewardship issue. And though it may be fun for you, it is holy to God. Though we can take any of God's good gifts and twist them back and run them through our self-rationalizations to soothe our consciences, it does not alter the integrity of God's Word. Not one iota.

I can say, "The 8 o'clock train will-not-come-will-not-come-will-not-come-will-not-come" all the live-long day. I can repeat it like a yoga mantra, and maybe, if I say it enough times, my mind will become convinced to believe the 8 o'clock train will not come. You may think what you want to believe, but please listen to this: do not stand on the railroad tracks at 8 o'clock. If you do, you will die. You can convince yourself that sex is not a serious matter all you want to, but you will not change this truth: sex is a solemn and holy concept.

I'm not just talking about intercourse. I'm talking about the entire romantic road that leads to sex. Unless the girl is a serial sex addict, which is possible in our culture today, she will not just jump into bed with any guy. Sex begins at "hello" for a girl. That line is from the movie *Jerry Maguire*. Jerry and Dorothy had a falling out. The night they reconciled, Jerry began his reconciliation speech, and Dorothy tearfully interrupted him by saying, "Shut up. Just shut up. You had me at hello." And then they kissed and made up.

Dorothy is normal. Dorothy is representative of most girls who allow their God-given wiring to function rightly. They are ready, willing, and able to be loved well, right from the first "hello." The onus is on the guy to lead well—from the "hello" to the altar, and into marital harmony, with gospel-motivated love being the one constant from the beginning of the relationship until the end. That role is the primary responsibility of the man in the relationship.

And then some will say, "We've messed up. What do we do?" There are two types of people who have messed up by engaging in some form of sex before marriage:

- Those who are not married.
- Those who are married and did it while dating.

To the Unmarried

The best-case scenario for those who are unmarried is for the couple to talk to each other about what they have done and to repent to God and each other. Then they should let somebody else know about what they have done. The primary reason to do this is that they have proven a lack of trustworthiness with each other and they want to pursue God's community for help humbly. They need help to work through what they have done, and they need help to keep them from repeating past mistakes.

They have violated God's imperative to stay pure. If they are humble and willing to submit to God, not only will they have a healthy suspicion toward themselves and what they are capable of doing, but they will desire godly care and accountability. The act of sexual activity before marriage is "exhibit A" that they cannot be trusted. If they deny this obvious truth, their initial foolishness of sexual activity will be compounded by future folly that they will most assuredly do.

"Can a man carry fire next to his chest and his clothes not be burned? Or can one walk on hot coals and his feet not be scorched?" (Proverbs 6:27–28).

The first people who they should talk to are their respective dads and moms. I'm aware that with the state of too many families, sitting down and having a biblically mature conversation is not remotely fathomable. In such cases, I would recommend their pastor or another primary spiritual leader who has been in their lives. If your boyfriend does not lead you in this area, you must lead. Don't incarcerate yourself in a relationship by marrying a guy who will have sexual activity with you, while continuing to fail in his leadership, as evidenced by not humbly leading you through active repentance.

To the Married

If you are married, I recommend for the husband to lead his wife through a discussion about their sexual activity while they were dating. It would not be wise or redemptive to gloss over this. It was a failure in leadership then, and it would be another failed leadership opportunity if he does not lead his wife through it now.

The husband needs to repent to his wife humbly. He needs to let her feel and experience his contrite heart (Psalm 51:17). He also needs to walk her through the guilt and shame of what she did. She was an active participant. Don't assume that you can ignore sin: it will always seek its revenge on you if it is not confessed and forgiven (Romans 1:18).

Additionally, he should walk her through any bitterness or anger that she may be carrying in her heart because of his failure in leadership. You must remove these hindrances from the marriage relationship. If your husband does not walk you through these things because he is still choosing to lead poorly, my recommendation would be for you to find help so that your conscience can be clear, you can cleanse your heart, and you can find release from what you did when you were young and foolish.

Call to Action

1. For the guy: To what degree and how have you struggled with lust or porn?
2. Do you need to repent to God and your girlfriend regarding your sexual/romantic activity with her? If so, will you do so?
3. What parameters have you put into your life to keep you both from engaging in sexual activity before your marriage?
4. Who is holding you accountable for these things, while bringing discipleship care and oversight into your lives?

Chapter 10

Premarital Sex

In the last chapter, I talked about the differences between boys and girls and their unique sexual temptations. Now I'm going to share the long-term consequences of premarital sex by looking at a couple who had fornicated and the long-term effects of their cover-up.

Mable met Biff in high school. Though it was not "love at first sight" for her, it was for him. He was smitten. They began to hang out during their senior year. They wrote letters to each other during college because they were three states apart. They dated for the summer months. After graduation, they resumed their relationship and dated pretty heavily right up until the day they were married. Their post-college dating relationship lasted two years.

Both sets of parents liked them. They were good kids. They went to a good church, and they caused no real problems for their parents. I'm not sure if it was because of their good behavior or blind trust, but both sets of parents took a hands-off approach to the relationship. The isolation left Mable and Biff with a lot of time alone, and no one was asking the right kind of questions about their temptations or how they guarded their hearts against the temptation to have sex. Their over-familiarization with each other and the assumed marriage-to-be tempted them to let down their guards.

Nine months before their wedding day they committed fornication. Though they processed it differently, they agreed on one thing: they did not want anyone to know, especially their parents and pastors. The embarrassment of being found out by others was stronger than what God thought about what they were doing. So, they kept it quiet. What Mable did not anticipate was that she could not keep her conscience quiet (Romans 2:14–15). Her inner voice was setting off a silent alarm in her soul.

"Therefore, as the Holy Spirit says, 'Today, if you hear his voice, do not harden your hearts'" (Hebrews 3:7–8a).

She struggled more than Biff even though she knew most of her girlfriends were doing it. This awareness seemed to calm the noise that was going on inside of her (1 Timothy 4:2). She also kept busy with her grocery store job. Whenever she became torn between telling and keeping it quiet, she rationalized it away. Her thoughts ran along these lines:

- "If I tell, I will be embarrassed" (Proverbs 29:25).
- "If I say anything, my dad may not allow me to marry Biff" (Hebrews 11:6).
- "We're getting married soon, so it will not matter" (Proverbs 28:13).
- "We only did it once, which is far better than most of my friends" (2 Corinthians 10:12).
- "How big of a deal can it be?" (Romans 6:23).

Layering the Conscience

When they met for premarital counseling, their counselor asked them if they had sex. Biff was ready for the question: like a good western street fighter, his finger was on the trigger. He quickly replied, "No, we have not." Mable nodded in the affirmative, hoping the questions would stop and the counselor would move on to something else. The counselor did move on to the next item.

While Biff didn't seem to struggle with lying, Mable had internal angst about the deception. She was relieved that they were not found out, though she had trouble with lying about it. The ease in which Biff could lie about the matter compounded their strained relationship. He seemed calm and unfazed. After their first session, Biff jumped into the car and smartly asked, "You wanna get some burgers for your folks?" Mable was still stuck on the deceit.

What she could not have known, but should have perceived, was that this pattern of low-level deceit and spiritual shallowness would characterize the next twenty-one years of their marriage. Only after their divorce did she gain clarity on the kind of person she had married.

His ability to lie and unashamedly transition to burgers and fries shocked her back to the reality of the type of person he was, but she dismissed it and quickly readjusted. It slowly began not to matter. The main thing was for her not to tell anyone the truth about their relationship. A few weeks later she did muster the gumption to talk to Biff about their counseling session. While she hoped that he would want to talk about what went on, she began to realize that was not Biff's style. He was dismissive.

He said that it was not a lie since they were getting married and that her dad already approved of the marriage. She began to wonder how that could be good enough for Biff—to the point that he could index forward as though the sex and lies never happened. The underlying truth about Biff was that he had hardened his conscience—the inner voice, the moral thermostat that God gives to all of us to help us discern and respond to right and wrong. His conscience was not as sensitive as Mable's conscience.

Whenever you choose to hide your sin, your conscience will respond with hardness. Unrepentant sin creates a layering effect on the conscience. It mutes the moral voice inside of you. The more comfortable you become living a lie, the easier it becomes to live with the lie. The side effect of this is that it becomes harder and harder to discern right from wrong. Like a broken compass, the moral thermostats of their souls were malfunctioning. Biff and Mable were doing this to themselves, though they did not realize it.

A Peek into Their Future

Most of the couples whom I see for marriage counseling had consensual sex before they were married. And though their premarriage fornication does not represent all their problems, you can typically discern a constellation of sinful patterns that are associated with and flows out of their unresolved and undiscussed infidelity. That was the case with Biff and Mable.

As I began to unpack their current marriage problems, I saw a cluster of issues tied to their past issue of premarital sex. The sin of fornication and how they handled it was the template for how they dealt with all of their problems for the next twenty-one years. Take a look at the list below and notice how the issues tied to their infidelity also applied to the issues they had after they were married. It was as though their sexual sin was a snapshot of how they would do life as a married couple.

- God – They ignored God to have fun—whether it was fornication or future sin, they marginalized the Lord.

- Communication – They did not communicate well with each other, especially about problems. Mable internalized while Biff was dismissive.
- Rationalizing – Biff quickly justified sin away, which angered Mable.
- Conscience – Mable had conscience issues by not dealing with sin correctly. Biff seemed to be impervious.
- Disrespect – She disrespected Biff for his poor spiritual leadership. Biff felt her disrespect but never connected it to his failures as a leader.
- Manipulation – There were many instances where Biff would freely sin to get what he wanted. Mable felt manipulated and devalued.
- Discouragement – Mable's ability to sin would always tempt her to be discouraged.
- Disconnected – Mable's low-level anger and resentment toward Biff gradually grew from that moment in the car. They became spiritually distant from each other.
- Ignorance – Biff's low-level ignorance and disregard for spiritual things would eventually break up their marriage.

Whether it was fornication or future problems, you can see some of the standard and destructive themes that characterized their entire marriage. Fornication was a red flag for how the rest of their lives would go, especially when it came to working through problems. Sadly, the desire to get married was more significant than their willingness to call a temporary halt to the marriage to fix their problems. Mable hoped that their sexual sin was an anomaly to how they thought about and did life together rather than a precursor to what their life would be like in the future. Mable was wrong.

When Sin Is Unconfessed

Their ignoring of the fornication led them to their versions of dealing with it. Because Biff's conscience was desensitized to and distanced from sin, he did not seem to struggle as much as Mable. She struggled in several ways regarding their unconfessed sin. Below is a sampling of a few of the twisted processes Mable had been going through for years to make amends for her teenage indiscretion. Most of these things were subliminal—more felt than articulated. As she reflected later: "I could not tell you what was wrong with me. I was bothered, but I couldn't put my finger on what was bothering me. After we met for counseling and I began to see how what we did over two decades ago was the beginning of a long trail of similar disappointments, I had words and categories for what was happening in my soul."

"Do not be deceived: God is not mocked, for whatever one sows, that will he also reap. For the one who sows to his own flesh will from the flesh reap corruption, but the one who sows to the Spirit will from the Spirit reap eternal life" (Galatians 6:7–8).

Here is a list of some of the things that Mable struggled with, as well as her commentary on them.

- Lying – "I tried to ignore what we did as teenagers."
- Guilt – "I knew we did wrong, but I was never free from it."
- Blame – "I blamed him and would punish him in subtle ways."
- Self-Loathing – "Sometimes I would turn my anger on myself."
- Anorexia – "Poor eating choices was one way I would punish myself."
- Atonement – "This was my way of paying for our sin."

- Anger – "My methods did not work, which led to frustration."
- Fear – "Then I would oscillate to wondering if God was mad at me."
- Repent – "I've never actually known how to do this."
- Forgiveness – "I've never really done that either."
- Freedom – "I do not know what that is."
- Hopelessness – "The way things progressed, it seemed too hard to fix."
- Manipulation – "I have used sex as a weapon to punish Biff."
- Mistrust – "I don't trust what Biff says because of how he regularly defrauds me."
- Cynicism – "I also don't trust God because He let this happen."
- Shame – "I've felt bad talking about it with God, Biff, or anyone else."
- Regret – "I wish, I wish, I wish, ad nausea . . ."

You can perceive the consternation in Mable's soul. Sin is real, and you must deal with it in biblical ways. Biff and Mable made a choice not to confront their fornication head-on. They lied to God, to each other, to their counselor, to their parents, and everyone else within their sphere of relationships.

They decided that they would use various forms of denials, justifications, and rationalizations to make things right, hoping to keep their secret undercover (Hebrews 4:13). Though they did fool others, they did not anticipate how they should not mock sin because it would take revenge on them. Sin will extract payment from someone. It must. It's an unalterable law: sin requires a payment, which is the triumph and glory of Christ's death on the cross. Jesus paid for your sins, and you may repent and accept the payment He made by His death on the cross.

Though Biff and Mable were familiar with the gospel, the seriousness of their sin never occurred to them or how they would not be an exception to sin's demands. All they had to do was run to the cross and appropriate the forgiveness that comes from God through His Son, but they chose another path.

Payday Someday

Unwittingly, they decided that sin could extract its payment from them instead of placing their sin on Christ and walking in His freedom. That decision caused irreparable damage to their marriage. Their trail of tears ended in divorce, which leads to my appeal to any couple thinking about getting married: what you are observing in your partner's life right now is a precursor to how the rest of your life will look—only it will be exponentially better or worse.

- If he is walking in the Spirit, it will be exponentially better.
- If he is walking in the flesh, it will be exponentially worse.

Do not think you are the exception to this rule. If what you are observing in your partner is unclear to you, seek wise counsel to walk you through your relationship. Biff and Mable met with a counselor for premarital counseling. It was more about checking the box than a God-centered, divine appointment to learn, change, and grow. They spent the rest of their marriage living out the superficiality of their premarital counseling. If your conscience is speaking to you at all, you need to talk to someone who is willing to ask you the hard questions.

"Faithful are the wounds of a friend; profuse are the kisses of an enemy" (Proverbs 27:6).

The side effects of letting sin have its way with you are a hardened conscience and dysfunctional relationships. Your conscience is God's kindness to you to tell you that you need to respond to Him. If you choose not to respond to your sin biblically, the hardening process will eventually stifle your joy and damage your relationships.

Call to Action

"So whoever knows the right thing to do and fails to do it, for him it is sin" (James 4:17).

1. What is the right thing for you to do right now in your relationship?
2. What are the hindrances that keep you from doing the right thing right now?
3. What do those hindrances reveal about you?
4. What do they reveal about your partner?
5. Will you talk to someone today about your next steps?

Chapter 11

Fornication to Adultery

Biff and Mable came in for counseling because Mable caught Biff in an adulterous relationship. She was hurt and angry and the most important thing at the moment was to care for her soul. There was so much to sort out, but the pain that she was experiencing required immediate counseling attention. Adultery is unlike most other sins because of the deep hurt it presses into a person's soul.

Adultery Is a Hate Sin

This sin has a unique aspect to it. "Normal" sin is between you and God. If your sin is adultery, it's not between you and God only, but it traumatizes another soul. And the complications increase because you're sinning against yourself: the two of you are one flesh. Did you get that? Biff sinned against himself, but the "himself" he sinned against was Mable because she is him—they are one, not two people. Adultery is a strange sin.

In Ephesians, Paul talked about how a lack of care for one's spouse is a way to hate her. Some may recoil at the word hate, but that is God's Word, not mine. The victims of adultery would not argue with Paul or God. It was the deep pain of hatred that this lady felt to the core of her being.

"For no one ever hated his own flesh, but nourishes and cherishes it, just as Christ does the church" (Ephesians 5:29).

After a few sessions, things began to level out, and Biff and Mable were starting to experience care, restoration to God, and reconciliation with each other. These things were good, but we had to do more. Part of the counseling process needed to have a preventative measure to it. I did not want them to go back to this place again, but to accomplish this, we were going to have to do some deep digging that would rattle both of their souls.

Mable certainly did not want it to happen again. So, we had to think about why it happened in the first place and how both Biff and Mable needed to change their views about God, each other, and their marriage. One of the instructive things that came out of this conversation was how the adultery was not an anomaly for them but rather a continuation of a lifestyle that had been in place for nearly thirty years. Let me explain.

The Complexity of the Sinning Victim

Mable and Biff have known each other since they were in high school. They both are in their late forties now. They began dating in their junior year of high school, separated briefly during college, and resumed their relationship in full after their respective college graduations. They were dating—off and on—for six years before they were married.

During this time they engaged in premarital sex, what the Bible calls fornication. I was not surprised by this, which is why I typically ask a couple going through adultery if they fornicated during their dating years. In almost every case the couple had indulged in premarital sexual sin. Adultery usually has a trail that can be decades old. Infidelity does not just happen. There are patterns, as well as a lifestyle, that precede the spouse hopping in bed with another person.

It was hard for Mable to hear how she was part of the problem and part of the pattern in her husband's life. While she was not responsible for his adultery, she was grossly irresponsible during the dating relationship and their marriage. Mable never made this connection. As noted by the title of this chapter, somehow she had convinced herself that sexual fornication and sexual adultery were on different planes and had no relationship with each other.

The Complexity of Intellectual Dishonesty

Truthfully, there is hardly a difference between sexual sin before marriage and sexual sin while married. Who wants to parse out those differences? It can be futile and wrongheaded if you don't factor biblical self-examination into the process. Somehow she had compartmentalized their fornication and recast it as love. The adultery, according to her lack of understanding, was another story altogether. She called it a sin, wrong, harsh, uncalled for, against God, against her, evil, of the devil, and a few other condemnatory things. I agree.

And all of Mable's descriptors about what adultery is apply to her fornication, too. Her guilt before God is no different than Biff's guilt before God when it comes to their choice to commit sexual sin before marriage. Do you think the Lord would say, "Mable, your fornicating sexual sin before you were married is not as bad as your husband's adulterous, sexual sin after you were married"?

There may be a difference in shades of black, but if you group one sexual sin as "better" than another, you're playing intellectual games, while trying to protect your reputation as well as a desire to hold on to your righteousness. Rather than Mable trying to set herself apart as a better sinner, lesser sinner, or not-as-bad-as-him sinner, it would be more honest for her to own what she did and seek to repent to God and Biff. And, yes, it would be wise, humble, and right for Biff to do the same.

The reason their mutual repentance is critical is that it is honest, and until they come full circle and deal with all the sinful sexual dysfunction in their lives, they will not be able to experience real, life-changing help. You can't divorce the sexual sin during the premarriage years from the sexual immorality during the married years as though they are not connected or mutually instructive. They are contiguous and progressive. Mable wanted to think that her husband loved her and that they were "making love" as teens.

She also wanted to think her husband did not love the adulterous woman the way he loved her: both actions were sinful sexual lust. Her husband was in love with himself when they were dating, and that has never changed.

Rooting Out the Painful Causes of Adultery

Mable needed to see the depth of his sin. It would not do for him to repent of adultery only. That would be removing the fruit from the tree but not rooting out the disease that caused the rotten fruit. The disease not only created the evil fruit of adultery, but the infection had been in the root system of the tree (his heart) for over three decades. It's the same disease that caused the rotten fruit of fornication. This reality will be hard for Mable to hear.

Her husband did not change into an immoral person at some point during the marriage, as perceived by his adultery. Her husband is not much different from how he was when they were fornicating together twenty-something years ago before they married. I wanted to spend adequate time walking her through the adultery before we got into the patterns that were in place that led to the infidelity. The pain of the adultery was challenging enough, but this was going to be more painful as she comes to terms with his lack of love plus her culpability.

"For the wrath of God is revealed from heaven against all ungodliness and unrighteousness of men, who by their unrighteousness suppress the truth" (Romans 1:18).

One of the hardest things for her to accept was how she had twisted her conscience to believe they were "making love" and not "making fornication." At some level of her heart, she knew this, but she was unwilling to admit it. She even began to discern why she did not respect her husband throughout their marriage. Her smothered disrespect was emanating out from under the truth that she had suppressed about the fornication. She thought she had hidden her hurt, which came out as disrespect, but she had not.

Repercussions for Suppressing the Truth

Mable had been "suppressing the truth" about their fornication all these years. She had twisted what they were doing as foolish teens by recasting it as love. But it wasn't loving. It was evil, and though she whitewashed over it, God did not. Paul said God reveals His wrath against anyone who suppresses the truth by their unrighteousness.

Mable may have denied, reframed, twisted, and republished her sin as "not-so-bad," but she was the only one fooled. She could not defeat the displeasure of God upon her soul. This response from God caused a backlash in her that affected their marriage. I have described Paul's text in Romans like a person squeezing a hotdog balloon. If you put pressure on one end, the other end becomes exaggerated.

Mable had put pressure on her conscience to reprogram her premarital sin with Biff. She was suppressing the truth, not realizing that she could not push it out of her soul. Mable had an "exaggerated soul" that was reacting to her attempts to press the truth down and out of her life. Rather than owning their premarital sex sin, by repenting of it, talking to her husband about it, and being fully released from it, they ignored it. But her soul was not ignoring it, and part of the backlash was the subtle disrespect and not-so-subtle anger that she had toward her husband.

Mable had become a critical wife. She rarely encouraged Biff and seemed to communicate steady displeasure toward him. Imagine how much could have been accomplished in their lives if they would have admitted their sin to each other and God and effectively repented of it. Perhaps they would have needed to get some help, but the embarrassment of what they did back then was more potent than coming clean with God and enjoying the freedom of a pure conscience. She chose to stuff it by relabeling what they were doing as love.

Consenting Partners in Crime

Biff did not love her. Oh, maybe he loved her to a degree. I'm sure he did. But his love for her was tangled and mostly an effort to satisfy his cravings. But before you think too harshly about Biff and how he victimized Mable, it's only equitable to see Mable in a similar light. She was a willing partner also. You must not miss this truth if you want to help them.

Biff did not rape her. She wanted to have sex with Biff. She liked the "Hollywood notion" of sleeping together, being romanced, and having a man to want her. Both Mable and Biff are self-centered people who gave tacit acknowledgment to God and their Christian faith. Yes, they are Christians the best that I can discern, but they are worldly Christians. God is not in the center of their thoughts or their lives consistently.

"Do not love the world or the things in the world. If anyone loves the world, the love of the Father is not in him" (1 John 2:15).

This rejection of a God-centered life is one of the reasons the adultery hurts so much. Mable was less concerned about God as she was working through her infidelity, and she was more concerned about how "he does not love me" and "how embarrassing this was to me" and "what will others think?"

Adultery is complicated enough, but when it happens to a worldly person, it accelerates to another level. If the victim of infidelity had a deep and growing relationship with God, you could walk her through the adultery with quicker success because God would be battling for her. If the victim of infidelity is similarly selfish as the adulterer, two people have to make their way back to God. While God is merciful to the hurting, He is also a God of justice, which makes Him opposed to both of them.

"But he gives more grace. Therefore it says, 'God opposes the proud but gives grace to the humble'" (James 4:6).

Mable can't play the victim card exclusively and blindly ignore the justice that needs to happen regarding her self-centered sexual sin. While she is a victim, she is also culpable in a marriage that has gone bad. She can choose either to suppress the truth of her sin while paying for it by experiencing God's ongoing displeasure upon her or she can confess her sin and let the anger that God put on His Son satisfy her sin. If she chooses the latter, many blessings will come her way.

113

- She will be free from her sin.
- Her conscience will begin to be more in tune with God's Word.
- The pains of guilt will disappear.
- Her self-deception will go away.
- She can find healing for the adultery without the complicating factor of her role in the fornication.
- Her anger, disrespect, and criticalness toward her husband will go away.
- She can experience a refreshing relationship with God.
- She can be a minister of reconciliation for her husband.
- Her repentance will help to cut the roots that have infected their marriage.
- She can model for Biff his need for repentance.

If she does repent, she will begin to learn and experience what real love is, while being less needy and demanding. If her husband repents, she will be ready to experience real marital love, instead of being two self-centered people.

Call to Action

If you are dating and you are fornicating, I recommend that you break up for a while, let someone know about your sin, get some help, and decide if you're right for each other. You're a fool to continue in the relationship without getting help. Don't think you're impervious to something like Mable's story. You're not. Mable's account is fictional, based on several dozen couples I have counseled who fit this account.

And women are reading this chapter, who may not mirror Mable's story precisely because they have not lived through adultery, but they did fornicate during their dating years, and things have never been right between them and their husbands.

While they may not be experiencing the pain of adultery, they are experiencing the numbness of a lonely marriage with an emotionally detached and preoccupied man.

If you are married, I recommend you let your spouse know what you are reading, what you think about it, how it has impacted your soul and marriage, and how you want help. Then make plans to get some help.

You must resolve your past. If it is not resolved, it will take revenge on your soul (as it probably already has), and you will not be the person whom God wants you to be. Do not be fooled: you cannot suppress the truth by your unrighteousness. God will press His wrath on you. Any person who hides the truth will experience internal turmoil and relational dysfunction. It's the nature of sin and the nature of God. Get some help today.

Chapter 12

Sex for a Woman

Sexual intimacy is one of the quickest indicators that reveals how a couple is doing in their marriage. Why? Because it is the most physical and intimate thing that they will do together. It is different from talking, dating, dinner, or a movie. Sex requires more. Sex demands more from two people.

You can do many things as a married couple and even pretend to get along, but sex is the litmus test. It is not unusual for a couple to attend church together for thirty years and be miserable in their marriage. They can pretend in the public domain but not so much in the privacy of their bedroom. People can be faked out, but when it's time for physical intimacy, there is no faking. Though a wife may do her duty sex and the man may be oblivious, the fact is that the marriage is on hard times.

Intimacy is either right, and your marriage is good, or it is not, and your marriage is in trouble. If your sexual life is disappointing, there is a reason: sin separates, and the bedroom is the most prominent place where you will discern this division. A good counseling question is, "How is your sex life?" or "Talk to me about your sex life." Fortunately, the Bible speaks to everything (2 Peter 1:3-4), so we do not have to go elsewhere to figure out what is wrong with our marriages.

No Sex with Layers

If you do not deal with sin biblically, the tectonic plates of your sex life will shift, and your marriage will be off kilter. You will be out-of-harmony with each other, no matter what kind of front you present. Sin is what happened to our first sexual couple. Sin entered the picture and division arrived. They felt shame, which motivated them to hide from the truth (Genesis 3:7). This one verse in Genesis explains eloquently, powerfully, and sadly why sex can be such a problem in marriage and why it is an indicator of the more profound issues a couple can experience.

Sex is as transparent as two people can be, and if the marriage is not right, one or both partners will begin layering themselves with fig leaves. When sin enters, the fig leaves come on, people start hiding from each other, and there is no desire to be entirely vulnerable, exposed, open, transparent, or honest with the other person.

You cannot have real physical intimacy wearing layers of fig leaves. If there is unresolved bitterness, anger, frustration, guilt, disrespect, unforgiveness, hurts, malice, or insensitivity in any marriage, one or both partners will be hesitant to become completely naked—vulnerable and transparent—to thoroughly enjoy biblical sex.

No doubt a man can be mean to his wife and demand sex from her. I am also aware that a woman can despise her husband and have sex with him. Hate or disrespect toward each other does not equal biblical sex. Biblical sex is an uninhibited willingness to unite with another person in God-centered, other-centered physical intimacy. God-centered sex is the most intimate picture of Christ and His church—thoroughly and comprehensively joined as husband and wife (Ephesians 5:28–30).

Biblical Sex Starts with the Gospel

Biblical sex is the height of physical/spiritual unity. Sin will not only alter this kind of intimacy, but it will reduce sex to a person's self-centered, self-satisfying, and self-serving cravings. Paul was able to bring the gospel to bear on all of life, which is why it is not surprising that he had so much clarity on how the gospel should shape and form our minds when it comes to sex.

"The husband should give to his wife her conjugal rights, and likewise the wife to her husband. For the wife does not have authority over her own body, but the husband does. Likewise, the husband does not have authority over his own body, but the wife does" (1 Corinthians 7:3–4).

You cannot read this passage without seeing the gospel orientation of what Paul was saying. The gospel—Jesus Christ—is all about going, giving, serving, and helping. Jesus was clear about His purpose and role on earth (Mark 10:45). He poured out His life as a ransom for others. The word Christian means Christ-follower: we imitate Jesus in all the ways that He taught us (Ephesians 5:1; 1Corinthians 11:1; Philippians 4:9). Imitating the Savior is not rocket science. We follow Him in all things.

When it comes to sex, we are to implement and fulfill the gospel's expectations. Sex is not mainly for or about me; it is primarily for my wife to enjoy. If she has a gospelized view on sex, she'll think similarly. The real question is whether I want to pollute the gospel by turning sexual love into a selfish pursuit. Porn is one of the worst manifestations of this kind of self-serving sex. Masturbation is another form of the me-centered sex worldview as the person satisfies himself (or herself).

Intimacy Starts outside the Bedroom

A poor sexual relationship is a symptom, not a cause. Though the symptom is inside the bedroom, the reason is outside. If you do not fix the real cause, your sexual experience with your spouse will never be right. Let me say it another way: if you are having sexual issues in the bedroom, sin is the culprit, and the first place you should look is outside your bedroom, where the sin is happening—specifically in your hearts.

Sex is an extension of who you are as a couple. If your intimacy is not right, there are things in your marriage that are not right. Your sexual life cannot be wrong and that be the only thing wrong with you and your spouse. Let me illustrate with an illustration: Suppose Biff slapped Mable across the face at 5 p.m. It is now 10 p.m., and Biff wants to have sex. Do you think Mable can freely give herself to Biff?

Though you may have never slapped your wife, it is possible you could have done things that have caused her to "put layers on," which has restricted your sexual experience. Some have said sex is a 24/7 experience for a wife and jokingly said it's about five minutes for a man. That is an ignorant statement. Physical intimacy is a 24/7, lifetime experience between a man and a woman. To understand this, you must know what is involved for a woman to be genuinely free to give herself up to a man.

Working without a Net

The best way to understand this kind of freedom is to know the conditions that must be in place in the marriage. She needs assurance in two primary areas.

- Do you love me?
- Will you protect me? (Or, are you safe?)

Think about your most vulnerable moments in life where you sensed fear or the possibility of danger. What did you want to know from God?

- Dear Lord, do you love me?
- Dear Lord, will you protect me?

If you know God loves you and you are aware of His protection (Romans 8:31), you can be vulnerable and free to follow where He leads. God has your back (Genesis 39:2). Love and security are two of the most powerful things a man can provide for his wife: give her your love and protective care.

God made Eve for Adam, not for Himself. Adam had a responsibility to take care of Eve, which he did by doing for her what God did for him: He loved her while providing a safe context for her to be vulnerable. If Eve sensed shame, guilt, harshness, frustration, disappointment, unkindness, or any other type of disapproving sin, she would have been reluctant to open up to Adam freely. Sin inhibits intimacy. Ultimately, this is what happened in Genesis 3:7.

Let's Go Farther

Have you ever played the game where you were blindfolded, and someone put a mystery food in your mouth? You would not play that game if you knew the other person did not love you and was not interested in your well-being. Similarly, a wife needs assurance that her husband is entirely in love with her and only has her best interests at heart. He is her lover and protector. This kind of assurance releases her to enjoy and experience love-making fully.

If she is not confident of your loving and protective care, she will have one eye on you during sex and one eye on her desire to enjoy it. She will be torn (James 1:5–8). At best, it would be a double-minded sexual experience, which is a frustrating experience. She will not have assurances of your love because of how you respond to her outside the bedroom. You cannot fake genuine love. If you love your wife, she will know it. That kind of love looks like the love of Christ, which frees your wife to close both eyes and take a fantastical, delightful trip.

The Love of Christ

There are several templates that we find in God's Word to give us clarity on what the love of Christ looks like in marriage. First Corinthians 13:4–7 is one such template. Another one that I like is what we call the fruit of the Spirit (Galatians 5:22–23). Galatians is the main template that I use to gauge how I think about and treat my wife. Nothing will remove the layers of reticence and send a wife into the freedom of intimate love like a man who is exhibiting these Christlike character traits. These nine questions are excellent to assess your "outside the bedroom love" for your wife.

- Love – Does your spouse see, experience, and feel your affectionate love?
- Joy – Is your spouse affected by the joy that you have in the Lord?
- Peace – Is your spouse affected by the peace you have in your soul?
- Patience – Is your spouse a regular recipient of your patience?
- Kindness – Would your spouse characterize your actions and reactions as kind?
- Goodness – Is your spouse a regular recipient of God's goodness through you?
- Faithfulness – Does your spouse find security in your faithfulness?

- Gentleness – Is your spouse relaxed around you, and does she feel your gentle warmth?
- Self-control – Does your spouse feel secure around you, knowing God is controlling you?

Practically Speaking

Imagine if your wife experienced this kind of love from you. The love of Christ coming through you would release her to be vulnerable with you. If you both are humble, I would recommend you talk about this chapter (James 4:6). If one or both of you are not humble, I suggest you find help because there are unresolved problems that hinder you from getting to a place of maturity to where you can have a "Christian conversation" about your sexual relationship.

The critical thing to know is that your wife must be free to be sexual with you, and if you are not treating her like God's treasure (1 Peter 3:7), your bedroom experience will always be less than what God intends. You cannot be snarky, mean, non-affirming, nasty, or unforgiving to your spouse and expect things to be right in the bedroom. If you make things right outside the bedroom, things will take care of themselves inside the bedroom.

One of the most overlooked aspects regarding how to make things right outside the bedroom is a lack of daily repentance in the Christian home. Most Christians do not clean up their messes: they do not know how to repent. Active repentance is the only way God has given us to clean up our messes.

Call to Action

Dear Husband,

Be a leader. Lead your wife. If you want her to respect you, act like Jesus. If you do not imitate Jesus, humbly, repent and remove the mistake, and begin emulating Jesus again. As God told Job, "Dress for action like a man" (Job 38:3).

That means, "Pull up your britches and be a man." Give your wife something to respect. Take a hard look at the character of Christ, as seen in the fruit of the Spirit. Ask God to give you the grace to soberly assess yourself. Find a real friend who will help you change.

Unless your wife is unregenerate or insane, she will love you for it. Perchance she refuses to change, you can still be right with God. Be a God-centered, gospel-motivated, Christ-loving, Spirit-empowered, Bible-informed man for the glory of God regardless of how she responds to or treats you.

Chapter 13

The Gaze Capturer

The discovery of a husband's problems with lust, such as viewing pornography, can be traumatizing. Typically, this new revelation is more complicated than a man just watching porn. Often the "lust problem" is expansive, including the softer side of porn that involves fantasizing over beautiful women, even those who attend your local church. Because this is such a pervasive problem in our culture, I have already devoted some chapters to a man's problem with sex and temptation.

What I have not done yet is spend adequate time talking about the other side of the "lust equation." Because women are different from men, it is not readily comprehensible for a wife to understand how even a modestly attired woman may be a temptation to the unguarded heart.

Some women can even think that sinful sexual attraction is an issue for the unbeliever and that Christian fathers, brothers, friends, and pastors somehow have insulated themselves from this assault on the soul. This kind of thinking postulates that those who "really" need Jesus are those who do not belong to the church, as though there is a holy barrier that surrounds the church building and all the men who attend that assembly.

It is imperative that every husband speak honestly about these matters by telling the whole truth about all the aspects of porn, which I believe will cause mature Christian women to be grateful and willing to live in more God-centered ways of thinking and responding. Sadly, too many husbands are not leading their wives well. And many mothers are not modeling modesty to their daughters. It is possible that the next generation of wives, mothers, and daughters will be even more unaware than they are now.

The enemy deceives us into thinking that pornography in the culture is their problem rather than ours, but that is not the truth. Anyone can be an object for lust. For example, if you dress sexy in public, you will be dressing sexy for the public. What this perspective means is that you can be a gaze capturer whether that is your intention or not. "Do not be deceived: God is not mocked, for whatever one sows, that will he also reap"—even if you're sowing and reaping unwittingly. "For the one who sows to his own flesh will from the flesh reap corruption, but the one who sows to the Spirit will from the Spirit reap eternal life" (Galatians 6:7–8).

Two-Way Street

Some women will read what I've said thus far as though I'm blaming them for a man's lust problems. If so, I have not been clear, and you have misunderstood. Each person is entirely responsible for the sin that he (or she) commits. Nobody is allowed to blame their immorality on others, on circumstances, or as a by-product of living in a fallen world. With that said, it's critical that you know how porn is a two-way street. It takes two people to engage in porn. The guy who is seeking a sexual object to satisfy his lusts and a woman who wants to be the object of his evil appetites. Remove either participant, and porn would struggle to survive.

Typically, when people think about porn, they quickly jump to the perverted guy problem, which is only half of the equation, which is why you must reflect comprehensively on this issue. I have talked with many biblical women who have given me vigorous and compelling appeals to write about the other side of the porn problem: the gaze capturers. Before I proceed, may I ask you a question: when I say "porn" or "pornography" what comes to your mind? I asked my wife this question, and she said, "Naked women."

She did not jump to the perverted guy problem but talked about women wearing no clothes. What she conveyed is the other misunderstanding about the porn problem: that it's only about the naked porn women found on the Internet, adult movies, and porn magazines. Thinking that porn is just a perverted guy problem or a porn woman issue not only narrows the interpretation of porn to something that misses a vital detail, but it reduces the Bible's impact on the real problem.

To understand the real problem, you have to go deeper than the outward manifestation of the problem. Looking below the surface is how we address all our issues: we begin in the heart before we tackle the behavior, which is why the Bible starts at the root of porn rather than the fruit.

"I say to you that everyone who looks at a woman with lustful intent has already committed adultery with her in his heart" (Matthew 5:28).

You cannot get into porn without first lusting from the heart. Porn participation is the overflow of lust-filled hearts. Understanding the underlying heart issue not only broadens the pandemic scope of porn, but it's an alarming warning to women everywhere: millions of husbands, fathers, brothers, and leaders are tempted to lust though they may never look at porn.

"Each person is tempted when he is lured and enticed by his own desire (lust). Then desire when it has conceived gives birth to sin (porn), and sin when it is fully grown brings forth death" (James 1:14–15).

A lady in a church building on Sunday morning is better than her being on the set of an X-rated soundstage, but her church building is not impervious to the encroachments of lust. And her role in our ubiquitous battle against the invasions of lust is just as critical in the sanctuary as it is at her swimming pool. Any woman is a potential lust magnet that can attract a guy because this kind of temptation does not isolate itself on the Internet.

And unlike the alcoholic who can take another route to work rather than driving by the liquor store each morning, lust is harder to escape. After you reframe the conversation from the behavioral problem that it most certainly is, you will be able to perceive how much bigger it is, while being able to fortify yourself in the fight.

Are You a Gaze Capturer?

Without dismissing the man's temptation to lust or removing all the responsibility that he deserves when he acts out on that temptation, let's look at the other side of this problem: women enjoy being observed, and they hope someone will find them attractive. God put an attraction gene in both the male and female. In Genesis 1 and 2, the concept of looking at a girl and being liked by a guy was God's design. Adam was the pursuer, and Eve was what he wanted. And it was good.

Then the man and the woman fell in the garden. Sin opened Adam's eyes in ways that he could never have imagined before the fall of humanity. And Eve walked in her kind of darkness, too. They both enjoyed their unique versions of lust.

- Adam wanted Eve for self-serving purposes.
- Eve wanted Adam to pursue her for self-serving purposes.

Eve's sin is why women are easily tempted to seduce or manipulate a man. For some women, it is because they enjoy the tantalizing power they can exert over a guy. I'm sure this is not an odd thought to you, especially if you contextualize that desire within the feminist's movement. Feminists like Eve hate the role of submission, which is why they rebelled like their predecessor. Do you believe this temptation to manipulate or gain power is exclusive to the feminist's lobby? There are millions of women who love God, but sin tempts them to manage the opinions of others by how they present themselves to others. These women are gaze capturers.

Providing a Conduit to Porn

- Do you secretly enjoy the power (perverse security) you feel when people notice you?
- Do you secretly enjoy the ability to control (perverse security) others by your beauty?

Just as darkness filled Eve's godly desire to be pursued and enjoyed by Adam at the dawn of sin, a post-modern godly woman can also be tempted by the pleasure that lust offers and the power it promises. More than likely you have not posed in a pornographic magazine or starred in a pornographic movie. But do you believe you are less guilty than the woman who does if you dress in a way that tempts a man to sin?

Consequentially, you may be less guilty, but if you dress in a way that tempts a man to lust, you are minimally acting as a conduit that feeds his passion until he can find more explicit satisfaction somewhere else. You can unwittingly cooperate with the porn star by the way you dress. My appeal would be for you to guard your heart against thinking the porn queen is the only problem in the battle against lust. It is possible for a church-going, God-loving woman to play a role in lust's victories.

While I'm not your judge, I would appeal to you to talk to your husband, father, pastor's wife, small group leader's wife, or some other godly person who is willing to speak into your life lovingly. If you are not dressing in a way that is alluring, tempting, manipulating, seducing, or gaze capturing, you have nothing to worry about and nothing to change.

But if you are, wouldn't it be great to know now? Wouldn't humility motivate a Christ-centered response from you? I realize this brings up a whole other set of problems in the Christian community about close, compassionate, competent, and courageous friends.

Who Is Your Faithful Friend?

"Faithful are the wounds of a friend; profuse are the kisses of an enemy" (Proverbs 27:6).

One of the sadder observations that I have made in the Christian community is the lack of loving courage that is required to bring the corrective care that this kind of problem demands. The proverbial faithful friend is more of an anomaly than a ubiquitous reality. Sadly, when there is wounding, it seems to happen with harshness and carelessness rather than corrective love that leaves the person built up in the faith. Individuals freed by the gospel act like the gospel. In the context of this discussion, there are two essential characteristics of this kind of gospel freedom.

- The caregiver brings corrective care in a spirit of gentle love that is courageous, compassionate, complete, and constructive.

- The care-receiver wants their corrective care because the gospel has delivered them from the desire to hide or self-protect.

If either one of those conditions does not happen, friends will not be faithful to each other, which brings you to two critical questions.

- Are you freed by the power of the gospel to be a loyal friend?
- Are you freed by the power of the gospel to ask a faithful friend to evaluate your clothing choices?

If you are free to ask a friend for help, I suggest that you press the point further by sharing with that person some of your temptations. Make it easy for them to care for you. Rather than expecting them to ask you the perfect question, you can circumvent this potential pitfall in caregiving by being proactive through releasing them from the potential of asking the wrong questions.

Hey, Good Looking

One of the significant tensions in the modesty war is our misunderstanding of what it means to look desirable. Usually, the point-of-focus gets hung-up on the word "desirable" as in, "Are you saying I should not look desirable?" Most certainly it is a good thing to look desirable and to want someone to desire you. That is living according to how God designed you. To be undesirable could be a hindrance to the gospel's effectiveness. The real issue here is not about being desirable, but rather it is about whose authority you are going to submit to as the definers of desirable.

Many women are not even sure what is inappropriate anymore. They have given themselves over to following the media, the fashion gurus, and Hollywood. It is a sad commentary on the church that our culture is doing the trendsetting within the church. The only people in the world with the right answers about modesty should be setting the pace and establishing the trends, at least within our Christian culture.

Call to Action

Now it's time to review what you've read. Here are a few questions for your consideration.

1. When you think about the porn problem, what is the first thing that comes to your mind?
2. Have you considered the source of porn, which is lust from the heart?
3. Do you realize how you cannot confine lust to the porn industry?
4. Because lust is omnipresent, what is your responsibility in fighting against its encroachments?
5. Because lust is omnipresent, what specific way do you lust? (Think about your cravings, sinful desires, or things that have more control over your thoughts than Sovereign Lord.) This last question may be the most important one for you to answer. Our most potent sin pattern is self-righteousness, which manifests by finding someone you can criticize. It's easy to compare sins with other individuals. Paul said, "None is righteous, no, not one" (Romans 3:10).

Chapter 14

Intimate Conversations

You know your marriage is stable when you can have sexually oriented conversations with your spouse. Outside of having intimate discussions about what the Lord is doing in your life, there is probably no other kind of marital talk that reveals the real strength of your relationship than conversations about sex and sexuality between spouses.

Though we live in a sexually explicit culture where promiscuous thinking and behaving is the norm, many Christian husbands and wives are still intimidated about having God-centered, biblically-motivated sex talks. There are many reasons for this problem. The main one being our "Adamic-inherited-fear" that impacts every sphere of our thoughts and actions. The closer you press toward spiritual and physical intimacy, the more difficult it will be for you to be vulnerable with others.

"And the LORD God commanded the man, saying, 'You may surely eat of every tree of the garden, but of the tree of the knowledge of good and evil you shall not eat, for in the day that you eat of it you shall surely die'" (Genesis 2:16–17).

The two fundamental breakdowns after Adam and Eve sinned in the garden were their relationships with God and each other. The Lord told them that if they sinned there would be a severing of His protective and sovereign care. Adam and Eve ignored His warning by sinning anyway, and the "fear factor" kicked in shortly after that. And humanity's fallen, fearful state is why some people are intimidated about discussing intimate things.

"And he said, 'I heard the sound of you in the garden, and I was afraid, because I was naked, and I hid myself'" (Genesis 3:10).

Adam and Eve became afraid of God. Their fearfulness not only affected the spiritual dynamics of their lives, but it also changed them physically. God became distant, and they became sexually confused.

"Then the eyes of both were opened, and they knew that they were naked. And they sewed fig leaves together and made themselves loincloths" (Genesis 3:7).

We're born with a sense of shame and guilt. We have this internally awkward awareness that compels us to want to hide from God and others (Romans 3:10–12), which is why there is a direct correlation between how a person relates to God spiritually and how he relates to his spouse sexually. The God-influenced man will have a healthy view and practice of sex (1 Corinthians 7:1–5). The same goes for his wife. The godless man or woman will have an unbiblical view and practice of sex.

Your perspective, attitude, and practice of sexuality are proportional to your worldview, attitude, and relationship with the Lord. Adam and Eve broke their relationship with God, which spun them into sexual confusion. Sexual dysfunction makes sense because God is the Author of sex. He created Adam and Eve for the enjoyment of each other (Genesis 2:24–25). Sex was God's idea. Then sin came, and their thinking about sex became chaotic.

Perfect Sex

I am going to highlight two areas where sin can easily break a husband and wife down while keeping them from being naked and unashamed with each other.

- Sin will keep a man from talking about his sexual temptations.
- Sin will tempt a woman to be offended by his sexual attractions.

Because of these two realities, many couples are never able to openly and humbly discuss how sin is captivating them. Even to the degree of keeping sexually oriented secrets from each other. Lust tempts the husband easily, and insecurity hinders the wife from engaging him in humble discussions about sex-related problems. A lack of "sexual communication" is a formula for secret-keeping, anger, sexual frustration, communication breakdowns, bitterness, unforgiveness, and resentment. I'm sure you can add a few more ideas into the mix.

If a husband and wife do not fight for biblically appropriate sexual discussions, they will never be able to realize the fullness of the marriage that God offers them. Sex is a deeply spiritual moment for two people who love God and each other (Matthew 22:36–40). When omnipresent God is ruling the heart of a man and a woman who are physically intimate with each other, they are enjoying the most profound human, communal experience possible.

Think about the sexual relationship between Adam and Eve before Genesis 3:1–7. It was God, Adam, and Eve with no sin to interrupt their thoughts or actions. Grasping such things is hard. The good news for us is that because of the power of the gospel, the freedom of forgiveness, and the enablement of the Spirit, we can come to a "close approximation of the physical intimacy" that Adam and Eve enjoyed before sin.

Lust Tempts Men

Before a couple can come to this kind of close approximation of physical intimacy, they must deal with the reality of sin in their lives. They must not ignore sin: it is real, and it is divisive. When it comes to sex, there are two competing interests vying for the mind of a man.

- He was wired to enjoy sex.
- Sinful thinking distorts his attitude toward sex.

This "sexual confusion" means a man must be honest about how sexual realities play out in his mind. It also means his wife must have the grace to provide a context for him to share his most precise thoughts about sexual temptations. Adam and Eve were controlled by shame and guilt after they sinned. God was no longer the governing and motivating power behind their actions. Sin ruled their hearts, which exposed their nakedness and shame in a wicked way.

The first thing a man must do to counteract the awkwardness about having sexual discussions with his wife is to fix any brokenness that exists in his relationship with God. Conversations about sex originate from the heart of a husband as he relates to God, not with his lips as he talks to his wife (Luke 6:45).

If a man's heart is not right with God, the kind of speech he has with his wife about sexual things will not be appropriate. Too many individuals miss this vital step. If they ever get the gumption to share their temptations with their wives, they usually do so before spending adequate time with the Lord. God must calibrate your heart before you start talking about your sexual temptations. Keeping in step with the Spirit means being like-minded with the Spirit on sexual things.

If the Spirit is illuminating and guiding your sexual speech, you should be equipped to engage your wife with the fruit of the Spirit—love, joy, peace, patience, kindness, goodness, faithfulness, gentleness, and self-control—when you talk to her (Galatians 5:22–23).

Insecurity Tempts Women

All relationships are about giving and receiving. I have addressed the heart of the "speech giver" (the husband) when it comes to talking about his struggles and temptations regarding sex. It is just as incumbent on the "speech receiver" (the wife) to have a right relationship with God so she can hear from the Lord as she listens to her husband.

One of the many blessed things about the gospel is how it creates an environment where two people can be honest with each other. The ability to be gracious and receptive about your problems reflects two traits that we love about God. He will not judge or condemn you when you bare your soul to Him. This truth was why the Psalmist could boldly approach God this way: "Search me, O God, and know my heart! Try me and know my thoughts! And see if there be any grievous way in me, and lead me in the way everlasting" (Psalm 139:23–24).

Wow! How bold is that? How encouraging is that? God gives you incredible confidence to be honest with Him, and you know He will kindly steward your problems. How releasing it is to be free with Him.

"Therefore be imitators of God, as beloved children" (Ephesians 5:1).

Imitating God in the realm of awkward conversations begs the question for wives: how are you imitating God as far as creating a context for your husband to be honest with you? Your approachableness does not mean he will be honest with you, but that is not the concern at this moment (Romans 12:18). You want to imitate your Lord by providing a context for your husband to be weak and vulnerable regarding his sin problems, whether or not he steps up to this responsibility. If you are not able to provide this for him, your first call to action is to repair your relationship with God.

The biblical word for insecurity is fear. Adam and Eve were insecure because of their broken relationship with God. Your instability is as strong as your relationship with the Lord. The God-empowered, God-centered, and God-motivated woman is standing in God's strength, and her spouse's problems will not overcome her.

Your husband's temptations will expose what kind of relationship you have with the Lord. If you've placed more hope in his ability to keep from sinning than on the Lord's power to stabilize you during disappointments, your strength will only be as strong as your husband's ability to not fail. If you've placed your primary hope in God, your stability will not be affected by other worldly factors like your spouse's failures. And you will experience the grace to bring restorative care to him when (or if) he shares his more personal temptations.

Call to Action

Perhaps you're not able to have these types of sexual conversations with your spouse. I realize there are many complicating reasons for this. If you're not able to enter into biblically centered sexual discussions, the first place to begin is prayer. Ask the Lord to do a great work of grace in your heart

(Proverbs 21:1). He is willing to do such things for the humble person (James 4:6). Lay out your soul before Him, asking Him to provide the grace you need to be a God-governed spouse.

Maybe your spouse will never change. I don't know. But his change should never interfere with how the grace of God operates in your life. Be daring. Ask the Lord to search your heart, and if He reveals any evil in you, repent. Be free from sin.

Second, begin to make plans to enter into a discussion with your spouse. Approach your spouse with grace and courage. Be like Adam and Eve when sin was not present with them. You can do this if you have removed your sin through the grace-effective means of repentance.

If your spouse is not interested in going further with you, be at peace. Be released from the temptation of a bad attitude toward your spouse. You've done what you can do (Romans 12:18). Maybe there will be another time or season for you to reenter this discussion. If your spouse is not interested in going further with you, ask the Father to bring a friend of the same sex into your life to provide encouragement and care for you.

Warning – This kind of attention from a friend should never be about your spouse's faults. Your communication should be about your maturing in the Lord. Don't slander or devalue your spouse before others.

If your spouse is interested in going further with you and your heart has been adjusted by the Lord, by all means, begin talking to your spouse. Use discernment, wisdom, and grace when you start sharing your heart.

Typically, in situations like these, the other spouse has not spent the same amount of time in prayer and reflection. One spouse is almost always "ahead" of the other, spiritually speaking. Never assume that you're in the same place or at the same level of maturity, willingness, or humility.

Be measured but courageous. Help your spouse. If you're the wife, you should come alongside him to help if he chooses not to lead you. My wife is my number one discipler. She is vital in helping me when I'm not doing a great job at leading the way. I praise God for the things that God has given to her and for her initiative to humbly share those things with me.

Chapter 15

Four Musts

Biff and Mable have pockets of silence between them. There are things Biff is thinking, but he does not discuss them with Mable. There are things Mable is thinking, but she does not bring them up to Biff. Though they say they love each other, something is missing in their relationship. There are some things they won't discuss. They've only been married for five years, but if they do not resolve these pockets of silence, there will be more than "pockets" in the years to come.

In a worst-case scenario, they will find other contexts to share their more in-depth and vulnerable thoughts. Rarely do people suppress things that are important to them: they crave someone for these conversations. If a couple is not willing to remove the barriers that hinder their relationship, the temptation to go deeper with somebody will find outlets to satisfy those desires.

Where Men Find Love

For the man, it could be his job or a hobby. Men easily find their identity in what they do. If there is a tension in the marriage, it would not be hard for him to mentally check out of the relationship and find fulfillment elsewhere, especially in his vocation. The forty-hour work week becomes a sixty-hour plus love affair as he climbs the corporate ladder. He can build a kingdom and an image to suit his insatiable cravings for a tribal identity. His wife does not have to like him because his work becomes his new best friend.

Another typical scenario for a man to find fulfilling reciprocation in his life is with the opposite sex. So-called innocent relationships at work can be the beginning of a full-blown adulterous affair. Though a man may not talk to his wife, he will more than likely be talking to somebody.

He knows that it's foolishness and that someone will find out about his sin, but his desire for affection, approval, and acceptance will drive him into the arms of another woman. The fires of lust will take a man over the cliffs of insanity. If he's more cautious or shy, he will find his affection on the Internet, where the cyber ladies are ready to entertain him. In his mind, it is risk-free, nobody has to know, and he feels somewhat justified because his wife is a nag.

Where Women Find Love

Women are no different than men. The desire for affection and appreciation is a deep yearning. If her husband ignores her, she will find people, places, or things to fill her cravings for love. Many Christian women find their Bible study mates as their replacement for relational deficiencies in their marriages. In such cases, her Bible study becomes her surrogate husband. Her female church friends meet the spiritual longing that she craves from her man.

Another common trap for the young mother is her children. She can feel a greater bonding with her kids than with her one-flesh union. The spiritual reality of her one flesh-ness is so disappointing that she chooses the emotional attachment of her children. She can easily preoccupy herself with her kids for the next twenty years.

Then there is always the possibility of adultery. Women are not uniquely insulated from sinful romance. The nonsense from the mommy porn book, *50 Shades of Gray*, is an example of emotionally hungry women looking for "sensual adventures of the mind."

Where It All Began

Biff and Mable do not want their marriage to go to some of those places I've described, but they are on the fast-track to relational dysfunction. They can't see it now, but if they don't fix their problems today, they will reflect on these issues ten years from now and know how they got there.

It always begins as little disagreements and other types of miscommunication moments that seep into the relationship. Like a hairline crack in the sidewalk, nobody discerns the magnitude of the brokenness in the years to come. When they first met as a dating couple, they could hardly separate from each other. There was virtually no silence between them and nearly total agreement in all things. Even the things they disagreed on did not matter because they enjoyed each other so much.

The season after the wedding, the drift started. The young couple began to take each other for granted, and the subtle separation began. It was hardly discernible, and whatever Biff and Mable did discern seemed to not matter because they were in love.

By the time they came to me, the hairline crack had evolved into pockets of silence and eventually a gulf of hurt that seemingly nobody could heal. If only they knew what to do about it when it first materialized. If someone would have come alongside them to help them. If only they would have listened.

The Missing Piece

Out of hundreds of married couples whom I've counseled there has been one absolute common denominator with all of them. I cannot think of a single exception with any of these couples. They all struggled similarly: they did not know how to repent. That's it. These couples did not know how to deal with the sin that came between them. Sinfulness is like those "grow animals" that you put in water.

You may have tried this. Our kids used to love them. They typically come in a dissoluble capsule to drop in a bowl of water. As the capsule dissolves, the animals begin to unfurl and grow. Sin is like that. But I'm talking humungous because sin won't stop growing until it chokes the life out of every relationship in the home.

If you don't take immediate, swift, and decisive action against sin, it will spiritually kill you and your relationships. That is what sin is supposed to do. That is the nature of sin. It is like poison in that it's designed to kill its victim (and you're the victim). Of course, this is why we have the gospel. The gospel is the serum that counteracts and destroys sin.

But this is the problem. Too many Christians either do not know how to apply the gospel to their sin, or they choose not to use the gospel. The specific aspect of the gospel that I'm talking about is the doctrine of repentance. Within this doctrine, I'm talking specifically about the four core elements that make up this life-changing, transformative idea of biblical repentance: confession, forgiveness, reconciliation, and restoration. Though there are several elements to repentance, I want to focus on these four.

Confession

An essential element of repentance is the confession aspect. The word confession means "to agree." The person who sins agrees with God about his sin. He and God are on the same page and in complete agreement about the sinful action. There is no doubt in God's mind that what you did was wrong. There is no doubt in your mind that what you did was wrong. You both agree there was a transgression. You and God are on the same page.

This idea is no different than any other person with whom you sin. For a confession to be true and real, there must be an agreement. When I sin against Lucia and confess that sin to God and her, it's essential that we three are one on this matter.

This perspective means that my confession cannot under any circumstances be a casual, "I'm sorry." A mature confession must have clarity and agreement. Lucia needs to know that I know what I did. I need to discern if she agrees with my assessment of my sin. If she doesn't, we must work until we do agree.

You cannot gloss over this point. If you are not in agreement, this will be the beginning of those pockets of silence in your relationship. You could go away thinking that you confessed, and your spouse could go away wishing you were more explicit about your confession. To agree is to be one. The confession must be a mutually agreed upon acknowledgment and understanding of what just happened.

If you do not confess properly, the residue of the sin will remain in your relationship. You will have an opinion about the matter. She will have a view of the issue. And you both will not agree.

Forgiveness

If you both agree on what happened, you can move to the next step: the offended person grants forgiveness. As noted, confession must not be a Christianized, "I did my duty" ritual. If confession is that way, forgiveness will be the same: rote but not real. You cannot go through the motions on these points. Sin is real, and transgressions will kill your relationship. You must dig down and get dirty until the offense is rooted out.

Too many Christians do the "forgiveness thing" while harboring the hurt, miscommunication, and frustration of what happened. This non-Christian approach to forgiveness is how a person becomes bitter and how sin kills.

Forgiveness should be transactional. You are making a transaction or an exchange. The penitent is guilty and looking to receive something from the person with whom they sinned. He's looking to obtain forgiveness: that is the transaction.

Reconciliation

If you do confession and forgiveness correctly, you will neutralize the sin. And if you neutralize the transgression, it will have no power over you or the offended. Repentance kills sin, but repentance misapplied will leave the effects of sin between you and the victim. As you can see, humble communication is vital here.

A misunderstanding and misapplication of repentance are the reasons couples break up. They do not understand how to repent, and they do not know how to apply the doctrine of repentance to their marriages practically. It's a lack of knowledge and application.

Biff and Mable cannot come together into a one-flesh union because sin divides them. Sin divides them because they have not done the right job of removing the sin. The Bible calls the "right job" repentance. The accumulative effect of unresolved sin issues will continue to divide them until the final division happens in their future, which is called divorce. They don't believe this will happen to them. They are naive.

I can introduce you to scores of former couples who used to think just like Biff and Mable. Sin does not discriminate, and if you choose to give it an inch, it will take your relationships to irreparable places. But if they decide to use this gospel-provided weapon—repentance—they can neutralize the sin that has come between them and move on to the dynamics of restoration.

Restoration

Now that they have neutralized the sin and removed it, they can begin working toward maturing the relationship. Before, the offense was a hindrance that interrupted and diverted them from working together on their one flesh-ness. Now, they have successfully removed the sin, and it's not a problem anymore. The transgression becomes a discussion point in their relationship, which is one of the most valuable roles Lucia plays in my life. She helps to mature (restore) me to Christ and herself.

Because the gospel kills my sin sufficiently, she is not tempted to use it against me. And God does not hold it over my head either. Now we can get down to the business of talking about what I did, why I did it, and how I can keep from doing it in the future. Lucia has a vested interest in this conversation: she doesn't want to be hurt again.

So, we bring up my sin and talk about it. I'm not sheepish about talking about my sin because God and Lucia have forgiven me. She does not become angry talking about my sin because she believes that I understand it—confession—and have wholeheartedly sought forgiveness. There is genuine reconciliation.

147

What I'm saying is the sin has no power over either one of us. Who is to condemn? No one. With my sin behind us, we are free to work on a plan to keep me from doing it again. How cool is that? (Ephesians 4:22–24). Sadly, too many couples do not understand or practice this fundamental teaching of our faith. This reality is ironic in light of the main point of the Bible, which is reconciliation.

Call to Action

1. Do you confess your sins consistently to your spouse, boyfriend, or girlfriend? If not, why not?
2. What are some of the hindrances that keep you from being vulnerable and honest with your partner?
3. What does asking for and receiving forgiveness look like in your relationship?
4. Has there been a time when you forgave, but you believed the offender might have been going through the motions? Are you able to talk about that incident now? If not, why not?
5. Are there pockets of silence in your relationship? If so, why are you that way? What do you need to do to overcome this communication hurdle?

Chapter 16

Competitive Communication

In some relationships, communication is more about winning and losing rather than understanding each other. Guarding hearts and harnessing tongues is hard. This problem reminds me of when Lucia and I are getting edgy with each other. It can be a challenge for me to guard my heart and harness my tongue (James 3:8). My first thought is not typically a desire to understand her (1 Peter 3:7), but rather to make my point as persuasively as I can.

This tactic is called competitive communication—a method of talking that contradicts the others-centered nature of the gospel (Mark 10:45). When the winning and losing mentality of our culture creeps into our Christianity, we will no longer be a united body but rather a combatant community. Winning at all costs is the survival-of-the-fittest attitude that comes from our Adamic instincts.

"The last will be first, and the first last" (Matthew 20:16).

I am not wired to be humble. My natural disposition is to be a proud, self-reliant man who likes to win. Winning is so ingrained in Adamic people that we cannot see how the thought of it conflicts with the gospel. Marital communication is one of those contexts where you can find a kind of survival-of-the-fittest competition. Like two soccer players colliding as they go for the ball, one is sprawled on the turf while the other races down the field to make the point.

Gospel-centered communication is different: it is about a towel and a basin (John 13:1–17). It is not about winning in the way that we understand winning. Ultimately the gospel does win but not through the usual processes that we think about victory (1 Corinthians 1:18–25). Even the Lord's disciples had a hard time grasping this idea of dying to win (Mark 8:31–33). They trained their minds to take the hill rather than helping their friend up a hill.

Corrupting Words

"Let no corrupting talk come out of your mouths, but only such as is good for building up, as fits the occasion, that it may give grace to those who hear" (Ephesians 4:29).

The cliché says sticks and stones will hurt, but words will never harm. It's a lie. I have talked with scores of people who have shared stories of being maltreated because of the poor communication dynamics within their relational constructs. Whether it is how a husband speaks to his wife, a wife to her husband, a parent to a child, or siblings talk to each other, the story is the same: when the gospel is not motivating your speech patterns, people will be hurt.

This problem transcends time and generations. It is common to talk to a middle-aged man who recounts how his dad's hurtful words affected him as a child. He shares these stories as though they happened yesterday. Forty years later, he is still working through what he experienced. In many of these cases, the dad was a professing Christian, which only compounded the problems by distorting the child's view of his heavenly Father. In his dad's efforts to evangelize and show off Christ to the world, he overshot his family, specifically his son, by not giving him the best of the gospel that should have been flowing from his lips.

"No human being can tame the tongue. It is a restless evil, full of deadly poison" (James 3:8).

Like soldiers equipped for battle, our words march off our tongues with the ability to build up or tear down another human. If these soldiers are competitors rather than redeemers, the battle will be lost, and the relationships will suffer.

- Are you a redemptive talker or a competitive talker?
- In your last argument with someone, what held your primary interest: making your points or understanding the other person's perspective?
- Are you more interested in the other person's view or making sure that you convince people of your perspective?
- Do you have a healthy dose of self-suspicion when you argue with your spouse?
- How does the gospel practically impact the way you talk to others?

Battling the Tongue

"Let the words of my mouth and the meditation of my heart be acceptable in your sight, O LORD, my rock and my redeemer" (Psalm 19:14).

Thank God for the gospel that tames our tongues because no person can. Our tongues are an unruly evil that we must subject to the gospel's power (Romans 1:16). This necessity is not a one-time subjugation but rather a daily ritual that we should enforce upon our mouths (Luke 9:23). We will not subdue our tongues ultimately until Jesus returns to give us new ones, but that does not have to be bad news. We have a gospel. An inability to tame the tongue is only unfortunate for those who do not have the power of the gospel resident within them.

Christians have this gospel power working in them (Ephesians 3:20). We can change. It boils down to two main things: do you perceive the need to change your tongue, and are you willing to do what it takes to reorient your mind to reshape your communication (Ephesians 4:22)? This process will not come easy, but it can happen for a person who has had enough of his or her miserable speech patterns.

God will give grace to a humble person (James 4:6). If you want to be a redemptive talker, the first thing for you to do is lay your tongue on the altar while asking the Lord to change it. This response to the Lord means your heart must transform, which includes your motives and attitudes. Tongue problems begin in the heart, not on the lips (Luke 6:45).

- Do you want to change?
- Do you want to talk the way Jesus spoke?
- If so, let's make a practical plan to change.

Redemptive Talk

One of the unique aspects of the gospel is the direction in which it points. It is always looking away from the subject and toward the object. The gospel has a predetermined interest in others (Philippians 2:3–4). Christ came from His place to our place so that He could redeem us (John 3:16; Philippians 2:5–6). This understanding is vital for you to know before you open your mouth. If you do not perceive and practice others-centeredness, the first words out of your mouth will not have the other person in mind.

Your Christ-centered goal is to redeem (help) the other person (Hebrews 10:24). The first way you do this is by practically applying the primary purpose of the gospel, which can begin by seeking to understand (Hebrews 4:14–15). What is right or wrong is not the most important thing at the beginning of a conversation. It is more important to understand what the other person meant. What is their perspective? Do you know them? Do you want to know them?

"For he knows our frame; he remembers that we are dust" (Psalm 103:14).

This concept is what Christ did for us. Before He changed us, He became like us. He "got" us (Hebrews 4:15–16). Isn't this one of the primary things you love about Jesus: He understands you (John 2:24–25)? Doesn't Christ's affection for you motivate you to change?

Listen Up!

"Know this, my beloved brothers: let every person be quick to hear, slow to speak, slow to anger" (James 1:19).

Christ did not come here to argue with me but to help me. His purposes are always redemptive. You see this kind of others-centered attitude throughout the Scriptures where the Lord is interacting with humanity. This idea is one of the beautiful things that I appreciate about the Psalms.

The Lord permitted the writers to express themselves, even when they were sinning. God always gives us time to speak. He does not fuss at or argue with us, but He chooses to discern our thoughts and intentions, whatever they may be (Hebrews 4:12–13). The Lord respects me, even though He does not always agree with me. He shows His respect by taking the time to patiently listen, understand, and know what is going on in my head.

Excellent disciplers call this the "data gathering time." The goal is always to get inside the person's mind. It is essential to see what they see, to know what they know, and to feel what they feel. Without this understanding, it is impossible to help them (Romans 12:15). Without this understanding, the other person will probably not want your help. Isn't this a fundamental reason you want the Lord's help? He can listen without condemnation, which motivates you to open up to Him wholeheartedly.

- How are you at creating a culture of grace within your relationships?
- Do you have a "way about you" that compels people to want to disclose their innermost thoughts to you?
- Can those closest to you be vulnerable around you?

Stop Competing

There are times when I am listening to a person, and I say to myself, *Wow! That's some whacked theology*. Or, *My goodness! We've got some work to do*. I do not tell the person what I think because that is not the most important thing at the moment. I don't want to be one of those "all about the truth" guys where correcting them becomes the main thing. That would be a mistake. You can nickel-and-dime a person to death and go away feeling good about yourself because the truth has been made clear—at least your perspective on the truth.

This attitude is why Jesus is so different: I do not feel like I am competing with Him. We are on the same team. He makes it this way by taking the time to understand me and, later on, by taking more time to reorient my thinking about how things should be. I do not feel His condemnation (Romans 8:1). I do

154

experience His patience (1 Thessalonians 5:14). He is not rude, arrogant, or sinfully insistent on His way (1 Corinthians 13:4–7).

He loves me when I am wrong (Romans 5:8). When I need to transform my mind on certain things, He gives me kindness and forbearance, which motivates me to change (Romans 2:4). Ultimately, I know He is for me (Romans 8:31). His way of serving me by how He listens motivates me to want to love Him as well as to change in areas where I need to change. Gospel communication is powerful. It strengthens relationships while reorienting those relationships toward God.

Call to Action

Will you write down all the verses below and do a homework assignment by applying them to the meaningful relationship in your life? Write out each Scripture and ask the corresponding question to the other person.

1. 1 Peter 3:7 – Do you think I understand you?
2. Mark 10:45 – Do you sense my desire to serve you by how I talk to you?
3. Matthew 20:16 – Am I a communication competitor or a communication redeemer?
4. 1 Corinthians 1:18–25 – What are some ways my communication is different from the world's speech?
5. Mark 8:31–33 – What ways do you sense Christlikeness in my speech?
6. Ephesians 4:29 – How do you experience hurt when I talk to you?
7. James 4:8 – How do I need to change as it pertains to my tongue?
8. Psalm 19:14 – On a scale of one to ten, where would you rate my passion for talking in a manner that blesses the Lord?

9. Philippians 2:5–6 – In what ways do you sense my effort to understand you?

10. Hebrews 4:14–15 – Would you characterize me as mostly showing sympathy toward you?

11. Psalm 103:14 – Do I "get" you?

12. James 1:19 – Am I quicker to speak or quicker to listen?

13. John 2:24–25 – In what ways do I need to grow and change as it pertains to knowing you?

14. Genesis 9:6 – Do you feel respected by me?

15. James 3:9 – What are some specific ways my words show respect to you?

16. Romans 12:15 – Name a time when you experienced my empathy. How did it make you feel?

17. Romans 8:1 – What do you experience most from me: correction or encouragement?

18. 1 Thessalonians 5:14 – Do you consider me a patient person with you?

19. 1 Corinthians 13:4–7 – When you put my name in the place of love in this text, how do I need to change?

20. Romans 5:8 – How willing are you to share your faults with me?

21. Romans 2:4 – How do I generally motivate you to change, whether good or bad?

22. Romans 8:31 – Do you believe I am for you?

Chapter 17

Orienting the Home

Biff is passionate about the Lord. Mable, Biff's wife, is joyfully following Biff. Biffy and Biffina, the children, are humbly submitting to their parents. They are one big happy family like they ought to be. They have established the orientation of their home as God-centered. Their family is an excellent picture for you to use to evaluate your home. Every home has a leader. Someone must be in charge while everyone else follows, as you see with Biff's family. What is the orientation of your home? Who's in charge? Who are you trusting to take the reins of your family? Who do you want to lead?

Start with the Husband

Husband, your agenda is straightforward: to follow aggressively after God. The Lord should be your passion, your goal, your life. If you love God more than anything else in your life (Matthew 22:37), you are not only pointed in the right direction, but you have positioned yourself to serve your family in the most useful way that you possibly can (James 4:6).

If you are leaning heavily into God (Philippians 3:13), you will be sustained and equipped by Him. If your wife is a Christian, she will more than likely follow you with joy. A woman would have to be insane not to desire a husband who is passionately in love with God, as evidenced by him practically being Jesus to her.

Part of your job description is to create an environment that compels your wife to follow you. You should be developing this kind of God-centered momentum in your home. If you are biblically "crazy" about God, your attitude, thoughts, and behaviors toward others will be consistently transforming into the person and work of Jesus (the gospel). Even when you fail, your passion for God will motivate you to repent quickly, which will reestablish the God-centered orientation of your home.

Who's on Point?

If your wife is not following you, I suggest before you begin to critique her that you take a fresh and discerning look at yourself. Before you think about whom she is following, consider whom you are following (Matthew 7:3–5). Who is on point in your home? If the Lord is not the point person of your home, you need to change the leadership structure of your family (1 Corinthians 11:1).

After a lot of living and a good bit of failing, one thing I have learned is that I cannot be trusted to be in charge of our home. My wife knows this and so do my children. I have put my sin on display in our home many times (1 John 1:7–10). Hiding failures in a family is impossible. It is no secret to my family how I can mess up things, which is why it's imperative for Lucia to know that I am not the leader of our family. She needs this assurance. She needs to know that someone more capable than me is leading our family. As you evaluate your home, let these two ideas guide your thoughts and discussions:

- Who is the primary influence of your family?
- Who do you and your wife want to lead your family?

God Replacements

As you think about the orientation of your home, who or what would you say is on point? Who or what pulls your family along? What defines your home? Whoever or whatever is on the point of your family is your functional god.

- Your work?
- Your ministry?
- Your activities?
- Your spouse?
- Your children?

These are important questions. Some may ask how a person in ministry could not have God on the point of his family. The answer to this excellent question is one of the sadder commentaries about the Christian community. It is no secret that the fallout rate among pastors is high, partly due to their inability (or unwillingness) to guide their families biblically. It is also true that the rest of us, who lead small groups and Bible studies, fail in leading our families.

Ignoring family failure can be easy. Being ministry-minded more than marriage-minded is commonplace. Some church leaders' ministry is a way of placing an ointment on the shortcomings in the home. There are also many women in horrible marriages who lead Bible studies. Being an example to their followers is not as important as filling a slot in the church. Their Bible study can become a refuge—their brief moment of sanity in an otherwise disappointing family dynamic. If you are ignoring marriage and family failure while pursuing ministry activity, what keeps you from dealing with your marriage problems?

- Is it your reputation?

- Is it your craving for security?
- Is it your desires for approval?
- Is it not a priority of your church?
- Is it because only one of you is interested in changing?
- Are you afraid to deal with the issues?

Anything that replaces the work needed to put Christ on display in your life, marriage, and family is idolatry. God replacements like these can suck the life out of what should be a vibrant, God-centered home. I have known many men in ministry who have undesirable marriages. Christians place these men on pedestals, praising them for their reputations and skills.

Other husbands and dads spend their waking hours chasing the dollar. The American dream has duped them into pursuing a lie. They want the right neighborhood, the right job, the beautiful wife, activity-centered children, and the approval of their circle of friends.

Too often, Christianity becomes a tack-on to their lives. Religion is a means to be connected to the right people while providing morality-based training for their children. Nominalism is a dangerous business. God is not the point or the purpose of these families, and the fallout is inestimable.

Clogging the System

Have you ever sat in traffic behind a car that was not moving? All the other cars were moving, but you were in the only stopped line. The person in front of you was texting. That is what a wife feels like when her husband is not passionately pursuing God. He is preoccupied with other things. The Godward momentum of her family gridlocks because her husband is not progressing in his walk with the Lord. When the man is not moving forward, it hinders everyone who is behind him.

In the movie, *My Fair Lady*, Eliza Doolittle was at the racetrack pulling for her favorite horse, Dover. Eliza was a lower-class, Cockney flower girl who was being trained by Henry Higgins in the ways of a proper lady. She was put to the test when asked to have tea at the track with some of the upper crust.

She did well until the race was closing in on the finish line and her horse, Dover, was not moving fast enough. As the horses were heading toward the line, Eliza, in a momentary lapse into desperation, yelled, "Dover, move your blooming arse!" As you might imagine, all the proper ladies choked on their tea. They were astounded.

Though a Christian woman might not say it exactly the way Eliza did, that is how many of them feel when their husbands are not submitting well to the Lord in the sanctification of their home. It is as though the wife is running up her husband's backside because of his lack of spiritual forward movement. If your marriage and family are stagnating like this, here are a few questions for your consideration:

- Husband, does your wife humbly ask you to follow the Leader of your home?
- Do you have a hunger for God and a desire to follow Him as your family follows you?
- Do you know how to lead this way?
- Are you embarrassed to lead your family because you feel like a hypocrite?
- Wife, how are you encouraging and motivating your husband to lead you?
- Do you nag him? Are you critical of your husband?

- What is he more aware of regarding your responses to him: your critique and nagging or your encouragement and motivation?
- Can you and your spouse talk about leadership failure in your home?

Talking about Leadership Failure

The first step in reorienting your home to God is to be able to speak about what is wrong with it. You will not be able to do this without the humbling power of the gospel working in both of your hearts. If you cannot talk about what has gone wrong in your marriage, you will need a gospel reorientation of the heart so that you can have a gospel reorientation in your marriage and family.

Only humble people can talk about what is wrong with them. Couples who cannot honestly and humbly share their faults and failures have drifted far from the truths proclaimed on Golgotha's hill. A man or woman who knows where he or she came from has nothing to prove, nothing to hide, and nothing to protect (1 Timothy 1:15).

The gospelized person is not afraid of what others may know about him because he is resting in this truth: "I was once a lost sinner, but now I am saved. I am the Lord's beloved child, and His approval is all I need. By grace, God saved me. I do not fear what others think about me or what they may say about me. God has declared me free, not guilty, and pleasing to Him. The works of Christ define me." (See Romans 3:23; Ephesians 2:8–9; Mark 1:11; Hebrews 11:6, and Proverbs 29:25.)

- What hinders you from talking about how each of you has failed the marriage?

- Husband, will you address your failures without attaching her failures to yours?
- Will you humbly ask your wife how you can lead her more effectively?
- Wife, will you address your failures without justifying or defending them?
- Will you humbly let him know how he can lead you more effectively?

The two most common misapplications regarding the orientation of the home concept are the child-centered home and the passive husband.

Child-Centered – Some families put their children on the point of the home. Everything centers around the kids. The typical mom in the child-centered home can spend ten to fifteen years of her life in a minivan, caving to the culture's expectations for children, which is to cart them around and keep them activity-centered.

These children become increasingly self-centered as life revolves around what they want to do. They rarely learn humility, respect, and submission. They are also typically weak when it comes to serving others. They don't know how to serve because it's not their habit (Mark 10:45).

Passive Husband – Another common problem in a family gone wrong is the spiritually passive male. The passive husband home is where the wife takes on more of the spiritual leadership, while the man is preoccupied with other things that feed his self-centered preferences.

The child-centered, passive-husband home is upside down. Typically, the child and the dad are in the same home since the lazy dad opens the door for the child to be the center of attention.

Most parents don't realize the monster they are creating until the child becomes a teenager.

Call to Action

If the orientation of your home focuses on the wrong person or things, please understand there is no way to correct what is wrong unless you both are willing to sit down and talk about it and make a practical plan to change.

If you cannot talk about what's wrong, I appeal to you to find someone who can walk with you through the problems in your home. The incorrect orientation of the home rarely autocorrects itself. If it continues, the future fallout will break your heart. There is only one right way for the home to function: the Lord must lead, and everyone else must practically follow His leadership.

1. Will you talk about the questions put forth in this chapter?
2. Will you set aside some time to talk about your marriage?
3. If not, will you find someone to help you and your spouse?
4. Are you in a church that values your marriage over your ministry?
5. If only one of you is willing to make changes, will you begin making those changes today?

Chapter 18

Leading Husbands

The words husband and leader are synonyms. To be one is to be the other. The question that you never enter into the discussion is whether or not a husband is a leader. The more relevant and practical matter to talk about is the kind of leader the husband is.

Just as water finds its level, each husband will eventually gravitate to his unique leadership style. This concept is what happened to Biff. He came to his level. He settled into the person who he has always been, which was a surprise to Mable after they were married because he was not like that in the beginning. During their dating relationship, they had lots of fun, hung out with friends, and went everywhere. After they married, their lives slowed down, and their days took on another style like working, living, and settling.

While dating, there were so many distractions, and Mable was so caught up in having a compliant boyfriend that she did not perceive how Biff's passivity would come back to bite her. He was quiet, and she loved to talk. What could be wrong with that? Mable was a talking idolater who liked to be in control, and Biff was a fearful idolater who did not mind his wife doing all the talking. The things we initially love about people at the beginning of a relationship can become the source of our greatest annoyances after we settle into the relationship. This reality was the case with Biff and Mable.

Today, Mable is bitter while Biff's passivity has taken on another tone: he's passively bitter and angry at his over-talking, over-controlling wife. They have settled, though nobody is sure if their marriage can endure who they are. Nothing will draw out the best and worst in two people than putting them in tight confines for an extended period.

Weak Leadership Styles

When Biff and Mable came to see me, one of the things that I wanted to learn more about was his leadership style. Was he a good leader or was he a weak leader? Was Biff an active leader or passive leader? Was he a kind leader or a harsh leader? There are times when I have met with a guy, and he would tell me that he did not know how to lead his wife or family, which is what Biff told me.

According to his perspective, he believed that he was accurate in his assessment. I don't think Biff was willfully lying. He did not understand the nature of the problem, which is why I appealed to him to reframe his thoughts this way: *I am leading Mable and my family, but I'm doing a poor job at it. I need help. I want to change how I lead my family. My leadership methods are defective. Will you help me?*

Biff is like a lot of guys who give the leadership of the home over to the wife. It's the path of least resistance. It's also a huge mistake that can reap decades of accumulative heartache if not corrected. Even though Mable was functionally leading the home, Biff was still the God-ordained and God-accountable leader. Unfortunately for Biff, his leadership style was passive and abdicating because of ignorance, fear, and weakness, which compelled him never to change.

A husband who abdicates his leadership position by deferring to his wife will sow terrible fruit in his wife and children. Leadership failure was never meant to be God's design, but when it does happen, it never turns out well for a family. Biff needed to learn the difference between good and bad leadership styles. He needed to understand the impact that his weak leadership style was having on his family. We began talking through a few poor methods. I've listed ten of them here.

Though all of them did not belong to Biff, I did want him to have a better understanding of what he was doing to his family and how the long-term consequences were ruining them.

Ten Poor Leadership Styles

- The angry husband leads his family to either emulate or rebel as a response to his anger.
- The quiet husband leads his family to find other people with whom to relate.
- The weak husband leads his family to respect those who are strong.
- The distant husband leads his family into bitterness and relational disconnectedness.
- The absent husband leads his family into insecurity.
- The authoritarian husband leads his family into rebellion.
- The drunk husband leads his family into despair.
- The adulterous husband leads his family into relational confusion.
- The porn husband leads his family into their versions of self-centeredness.
- The workaholic husband leads his family to other relational connections.

Biblical leadership looks remarkably different from the poor styles listed. Here are a few characteristics of a husband who leads well.

Ten Biblical Leadership Styles

- The grateful husband leads his family into an awareness of God's work in their lives.
- The encouraging husband leads his family to be thankful.
- The sin-confessing husband leads his family into vulnerability.
- The repenting husband leads his family into biblical change.
- The praying husband leads his family to God-reliant attitudes and practices.
- The hospitable husband leads his family to others-centered activities.
- The serving husband leads his family into humility.
- The humble husband leads his family into God's favor (James 4:6).
- The Bible-studying husband leads his family into a God-centered worldview.
- The communicating husband leads his family into relational wholeness.

The one thing that these twenty leadership styles have in common is that all of them represent a husband and father who is leading his family. Back to the question: it's not about if you are a leader, but how are you leading?

Leadership and the Talking Male

Though all of the excellent leadership styles I mentioned are essential practices for every husband, there is one out of the ten that you tie to the rest, which is the communicating husband.

Poor communication is one of the most significant areas of neglect for men. Period. The noncommunicating (or poor communicating) male is one of the most inferior forms of leadership and the one that will have the most devastating impact on his family. God is a speaking God, He made us in His image, and one of the most effective ways we can image Him is by our willingness to communicate well with other people.

The fourth sentence of the Bible tells us about God speaking. There was no form to the earth, and God was talking (Genesis 1:3). He was speaking, leading, and directing. God is a shaker and a mover who leaves no one wondering what He is thinking. God has always led His people well because He is a talking God. In 2 Timothy 3:16 we see God speaking, talking to you. He has given you His plenary, authoritative, and all-sufficient Word, so you are not left in the dark about what to do next.

Imagine if God were a silent God. Imagine if He deliberately decided not to talk. Whenever we read about the silence of God in the Word of God, chaos ensues. It's like the years between the Testaments. A silent God is a horrible thought. Where would you go? What would you do? How would you know?

The Awkwardness of Silence

The characteristics of silence and passivity always lead to mysteriousness, awkwardness, and speculation. Mable said it this way, "When Biff is not talking, I tend to speculate on what he's thinking. I don't know what he's thinking. Biff never talks! I have to figure out what he's thinking, or let it go, which is so hard. That's why I'm bitter."

If your leadership style leans toward silence or passivity, let me recommend another technique, which may be a challenge for you, but don't give up; you can learn how to talk well. This issue is why I regularly encourage our children to speak often. It is far easier to "reel them in" from talking too much than it is to motivate them to speak at all. The primary way you teach any child to talk is to model it. You become a talking person in the way Paul told us to speak.

"Let no corrupting talk come out of your mouths, but only such as is good for building up, as fits the occasion, that it may give grace to those who hear" (Ephesians 4:29).

Talking to fill up airspace is not the goal. Your talking must be to shape and build up your family members in Christ.

- Are you the biblically communicating leader in your home?
- Are your words shaping your family into Christlikeness?

Faith Comes by Hearing

You cannot overstate communication problems. If there were ever a people group on the planet who had something to talk about, it's Christians. A Christian should never stay silent, especially in his family. Perhaps you're a lazy communicator. If so, you need to repent of your laziness. You cannot be a lazy man and expect to lead your family well.

Perhaps you have succumbed to the device addiction. One of the biggest deterrents of biblical communication in today's culture is our devices. Everyone sitting around the room on a device destroys redemptive familial communication opportunities. Faith comes by "talking and hearing" rather than by silence. Your wife's biblical trust will be built up by your words, not your laziness, passivity, reluctance, or silence. Maybe other things hinder you from leading your family with your words.

- What are those things?
- How does your wife contribute to your silence?

170

- How are you as a couple working against each other to where you're not communicating well?

The Gospel Motivates Biblical Leadership

One of the interesting things I noticed after a few meetings with Biff and Mable is that Biff was an excellent talking leader in other spheres of his life. There were some things he liked to do, and he did not show an inhibition about speaking with others. He was not universally passive or quiet—just around his wife. Isn't that the way it generally goes? Biff's problem was not that he could not lead or speak well. It was not a capacity or ability issue but rather a character issue: he could direct his family well if he wanted to guide them.

Biff's problem was in his heart more than in his behaviors. That was the good news. If his problem were an organic, capacity issue, there would be God-imposed limitations that would keep him from leading his family in biblical communication. Fortunately for Biff, he was not hindered by such things. He could change. The real issue for Biff was that he had not been sufficiently affected by the gospel. His sanctification was lagging behind what it should be. There was not a proper formation of Christ inside of Biff. Though he was growing in Bible knowledge and was busy in church ministries, his marriage was not being affected by the gospel.

Biff had to decide if he was going to emulate Christ where it mattered—in his home. The gospel is an others-centered adventure that begins in a person's heart and works out in his closest and most important relationships. If you jump over those relationships to live out the gospel before people who are not the closest to you, it's not a broken gospel, but it's your heart. It is a character flaw. It's a repent-able offense. The gospel practically lived out effects everyone in its path. Like a storm, if you're near it, you'll be affected by it.

Biff was quenching the gospel's power in his family. Though he came to me because of his broken relationship with his wife, he began to see that his more significant problem was a fractured relationship with his Savior. His relationship with his wife and children would only change in direct proportion to his functional relationship with Christ. You cannot lead like Christ if you don't authentically act like Christ. Biff had to choose if he was going to be a Christian church attendee or a man affected by Jesus.

Call to Action

1. What kind of communicating leader are you?
2. Will you ask your spouse about these things? (If you're the wife, this content applies to you, too. Will you ask your husband?)
3. Do you create an environment of grace with your spouse that encourages honest, transparent, vulnerable, redemptive, and reciprocal communication?
4. What do you need to change? How do you need to change?

Chapter 19

Biblical Wives

A wife can be a husband's most significant asset or his most significant liability. I think most of us know this, but I wonder how many wives have thought through how to be an asset to their husbands by humbly coming alongside them while submitted to them. Though your calling is to a particular role of submission in the marriage, it does not mean you can't be a Christlike example to your husband. Because you are ontologically equal to him, though submitted in your role as a wife, may I ask you a couple of questions about how you humbly come alongside your husband by your Christlike example (Ephesians 5:1)?

- How are you using your gifts, strengths, skills, and talents to help your husband be a better leader (1 Corinthians 12:21)?
- How are you using your God-given insights and wisdom to serve your husband (Philippians 4:9)?

I have often asked these questions to wives. Here are three of the more common responses that I typically receive.

- Humble answer – "I didn't know I could help him lead. Tell me more."
- Not so humble response – "Why does he need me to help him do what he is supposed to be doing?"

- Second not so humble response – "Why are you putting the weight of his failures in my lap?"

Let me tackle the third response first: if he has failures, they are between him and God. Each of us has a moral responsibility to God not to sin. My questions about you being a Christlike example were not about your being culpable regarding what he is doing wrong but about your living out the gospel because that is your calling. Though Christ was not responsible for your sin, He made a deliberate choice to come alongside you to help you while you were sinning.

"But God shows his love for us in that while we were still sinners, Christ died for us" (Romans 5:8).

The question in view here is not about tallying up the faults in the marriage. Jesus saw a need and knew that He could meet it. That is why He humbled Himself to the cross (Luke 9:23). You had a problem, and He wanted to help you with your situation. You recall the story in the Bible about the good Samaritan. It carries a similar idea.

"But a Samaritan, as he journeyed, came to where he was, and when he saw him, he had compassion. He went to him and bound up his wounds, pouring on oil and wine. Then he set him on his own animal and brought him to an inn and took care of him. Which of these three, do you think, proved to be a neighbor to the man who fell among the robbers? He said, 'The one who showed him mercy.' And Jesus said to him, 'You go, and do likewise'" (Luke 10:33–37).

The point of the story is that when we see a need, we should seek to fill that need if we can. This man saw a need and decided to set aside his plans for the day so that he could help a fellow struggler. One of the most profound demonstrations and motivating examples of the gospel in a marriage is when a wife is willing to set aside what she wants out of the relationship so that she can help her husband to become a better leader. Isn't this what the Savior did for us?

"Have this mind among yourselves, which is yours in Christ Jesus, who, though he was in the form of God, did not count equality with God a thing to be grasped, but emptied himself, by taking the form of a servant, being born in the likeness of men. And being found in human form, he humbled himself by becoming obedient to the point of death, even death on a cross. Therefore God has highly exalted him and bestowed on him the name that is above every name. in heaven and on earth and under the earth, and every tongue confess that Jesus Christ is Lord, to the glory of God the Father" (Philippians 2:5–11).

Jesus set aside the life He enjoyed with the Father to come to earth to help you become what you couldn't become on your own. Now you are being called to model what the Savior modeled for you (1 Peter 2:21). The Father is appealing to you to set aside your preferences for the greater good of others: "Do nothing from rivalry or conceit, but in humility count others more significant than yourselves" (Philippians 2:3).

The Savior's death was not the end of the story. Eventually, He was highly exalted to His former position with the Father. Because of His sacrificial work on the cross, there will be a day when He will be able to thoroughly enjoy the fruit of His sacrifice with millions of people who have accepted His finished work (Hebrews 12:2).

It's so easy for us to lose this gospel perspective and challenge, especially when the demands of the day or the disappointments of others begin to drain the joy of Christ from our souls. Losing this kind of gospel-centered focus is especially tempting when a husband is a royal knucklehead. The dawning reality that a husband is not what the wife hoped for can be overwhelming to the wife. Perhaps she spent her childhood thinking about her prince, and then she found him, only to be surprised that he is not as princely as she had hoped.

That kind of disappointment can circumvent biblical clarity and gospel initiatives. Instead of working toward maturing the marriage through her humility and Christlike example, her desire for something better overpowers her will. It's a natural trap.

You Don't Know Him

The most common response to my gospel appeal runs along the lines of, "You don't know my husband." Of course, that would be correct. I don't know him, and I don't live with him day-to-day like you do. But I do know that if he is like me, then he is selfish. He also sins. And he can be insensitive and stubborn at times, too, if he is similar to the way that I am. You're right: I do not know your husband. But let me ask you this: do you sin in response to your husband's behaviors? If you answered yes, then that is where you need to start modeling Christ before your husband.

Nobody can make a biblical case for sinning against another person regardless of what they do. Perchance you do sin against your husband because of his sins, you have found the right place where you can begin helping him. You can do that through the humble confession of your sin, which is followed up by asking for his (and God's) forgiveness. I'm sure that he needs to repent of something, too, but how beautiful would it be if you led him by your example of repentance?

Isn't this how you parent your children (1 Corinthians 11:1)? You teach them through your example. A picture is worth a thousand words. Imagine what a clear picture the humble Christ would look like to someone who desperately needs to see Him practically presented—someone like your husband. God has used my wife's gifts and strengths repeatedly throughout our marriage to help me to be a better husband. She has been a remarkable, practical example of what I see Christ doing in Philippians chapter two: He temporarily set aside His comfort for the betterment of others.

She has on many occasions set aside her preferences to help me understand a more productive understanding of Christ. In turn, this has simultaneously convicted me of sin, while it motivated me to be a better leader in our home.

He Won't Change

Then someone will say, "What if I do all this, and my husband does not change?" You're a realist who may be right. There is a high probability that he will not change, but that should not be the first question you must ask. The first question you need to ask yourself is, "Why am I doing this?"

- Are you modeling Christ before your husband primarily because you want him to change?
- Are you modeling Christ before your husband because you want to honor God regardless of what your husband does?

The unchanging husband is a typical scenario. There are many marriages where that is the case. There is a story in the Bible about a young, rich man who would not change either. When he encountered Jesus, he was told to sell all he had and follow Christ. Here is how the young rich man responded to the Savior. "But when he heard these things, he became very sad, for he was extremely rich" (Luke 18:23).

I do not know what happened to this young rich man. The Bible does not tell us. We do know what happened to Jesus though. He kept being Jesus. Even when some of those around Him would not change, He kept doing Jesus things. God gives grace to the humble, and if you walk in the humility of Jesus, even when you are not getting all you want, you will repeatedly be surprised by His grace (James 4:6).

I wish I could tell you something different, but I can't. I talk to people every week who want better marriages or better children or better parents. Sometimes it does not work out the way they want. That is the reality of the world in which we live. But there are things you can do, even when others will not cooperate. I had a friend give me a piece of advice in 1989, and I have never forgotten it. He said, "I can't make you love me, but you can't stop me from loving you."

He told me this at a time when I desperately wanted someone to change their mind about our relationship. That person never changed her mind, and I felt the helplessness of my unchangeable situation. My friend's advice was accurate. It became invaluable, and I have used it many times since. He was communicating with me another aspect of the gospel. You could say it this way: "God so loved the world that He determined to love the world even if the world did not reciprocate. His love was so profound that He gave His one and only Son to save a bunch of unlovable people. And by doing this, He left the door open for anyone to accept His love. If they did, great. If they did not receive His sacrificial work, their rejection would not alter His love for them" (John 3:16 paraphrase).

Your Real Motive

The first question you will have to ask is why do you want to help your husband? Do you want to come alongside him so that you can have a great marriage? That is a good desire. It's a biblical one, though it's not the best reason to serve him this way. Do you want to lovingly help him because you want to make God's name great? Now that is the best reason. If God's fame is not your primary motive, you will need to do some heart work before you go to the practical steps of working on your marriage.

You will need to spend time with your Father to get your heart adjusted for the challenging task ahead. Do not skip this vital step. Ask God to give you the grace you need to love an unlovable person. He will provide you with that grace if you ask with the right motive.

"You ask and do not receive, because you ask wrongly, to spend it on your passions" (James 4:3).

God can see in the darkness of your heart. He precisely knows what your thoughts, intentions, and motives are. You can fool others, but you won't trick Him. How you think and what you want are not hidden from Him.

"And no creature is hidden from his sight, but all are naked and exposed to the eyes of him to whom we must give account" (Hebrews 4:13).

If you believe that what I am asking you to do is a more significant burden than you can carry, appeal to someone from your local church to help you both. Don't be afraid to seek help. You will not be dishonoring your husband if you find support for your marriage. It's another way you can model Christ to him. It's a way to respect your one flesh covenant. If you have humbly appealed to him to change and he has not, let him know you're going to talk to a leader at your church about these matters. You would not be sinning if you choose this course of action. By all means, help him.

Call to Action

1. What is the state of your relationship? Are you getting better each day, week, month, and year? Or are you regressing?
2. In what way have you contributed to your relationship negatively? Will you make a plan to change yourself today?
3. As you think about your motive for a better relationship, which is more important: changing yourself, hoping it will make your relationship better, or changing yourself for God's fame, regardless of the relational outcome?

Chapter 20

Deciding Together

Biblical decision-making is not that difficult if you are the only one making the decision. There are challenges, of course, but it's much easier if you're the only one affected by the decision. Once the number of affected people to the decision-making process increases, the more challenging it will be to navigate with humility while keeping from sinful reactions.

Welcome to Marriage

When two singles become one flesh, decision-making changes dramatically. Because the married couple is "one person" seeking to put Christ on display in every way, it is essential that they work through the process of deciding things with God-glorifying goals in mind. They are partners, equally responsible to each other and God for what they choose to do and for how they work through decision-making. In this chapter, I'm providing a few general and biblical guidelines that can serve any couple when they are working through a decision.

If you are not married yet, you can use these thoughts by adapting my application questions with anyone who is collaborating with you on the decision. I recommend that you take the time to answer all of the questions after each section. If you are married, it will be an excellent opportunity for you to work together. This chapter will make a great date night.

You Cannot Sin

Regardless of the issues discussed or the particulars involved in the decision, there is no situation where it would be appropriate for either partner to sin during or after the process. This mandate is not only common sense, but it's biblical. Once sin infringes on what you're trying to do, you will have a hard time coming to the right decision until you remove the "blurring effect" of the sin. Sin clutters the mind and clouds judgment. It cannot be part of the process.

If a spouse chooses to sin, the most immediate item on the agenda at that point is to repent. Removing the sin is more critical than the decision you're attempting to make. You should not move forward until you take care of the division that is in your one-flesh union. Two people cannot work together on anything while divided. You must fully restore the one-flesh division so that you can get back to the business of decision-making. If someone chooses not to repent, it will be even more difficult to agree. This outcome creates three problems, where only one previously existed.

- Problem One: The decision you were trying to make.
- Problem Two: You introduced sin into the conversation, which divided you.
- Problem Three: Your lack of full repentance keeps you divided.

Refusing to discuss what has divided you is called a complicating matter—it "piles on" or complicates the decision-making process. If you do not remove this problem, it could be analogous to trying to swim with leg weights around your ankles.

- Are you working through a decision in your relationship?

- Are there any tensions or unresolved issues between you and your spouse?
- Can you bring up your tension and get things out in the open so that you can reconcile?
- Are you generally characterized as a quick and willing repenter? If not, why not?

Decisions Should Not Take Long

There could be something wrong with a relationship if it takes a long time to conclude a matter. Perhaps you're not going to act on what you decided for a few months or even years, but the actual decision-making process should not take that long after you have all the data. If someone is holding out by refusing to agree, it does not necessarily mean the hesitant spouse is wrong. Maybe the one who wants to move forward is wrong, and the one holding out is in the right.

Holding out and not moving forward sometimes can be God's kindness to the one who wants to get on with it. Perhaps God is keeping the couple from making a dumb decision they would regret for many years to come. Jesus's sober warning about self-awareness is critical.

"Why do you see the speck that is in your brother's eye, but do not notice the log that is in your own eye? Or how can you say to your brother, 'Let me take the speck out of your eye,' when there is the log in your own eye? You hypocrite, first take the log out of your own eye, and then you will see clearly to take the speck out of your brother's eye" (Matthew 7:3–5).

- How difficult is it for you to acknowledge that you are wrong?
- Are you willing to entertain the thought that your spouse could be right?

- Will you clearly articulate your spouse's position? Do you understand what they are saying?
- What are the good points about the other person's position?

Borrow Brains

"Where there is no guidance, a people falls, but in an abundance of counselors, there is safety" (Proverbs 11:14).

While there can be confusion in a multitude of counselors, there most certainly can be safeness if you choose to talk to someone outside of your marriage. Every person (or couple) should have at least one other person whom they can bounce things off for clarity's sake. Helping people with problems is what God has called all Christians to do for each other. Though you would not necessarily ask for advice on everything you do, it is a humble thing to reach out to someone who has the wisdom and breadth of knowledge to speak into your life.

- Do you have a trusted friend who can advise you about your decision?
- What are the advantages of talking to someone else about your decision?
- What would hinder you from talking to someone else?

The Husband Is Not a Dictator

The husband and wife are a team who balance each other out for God's glory and their mutual benefit. There have been many times when my wife has appealed to me because her conscience was not coming to terms with some of the decisions that I was thinking about making. In those situations, I listened to her appeals. Why?

- My wife is a Christian.

- She loves God.
- She has the Spirit of God inside her.
- She reads her Bible.
- She has a vibrant relationship with Jesus Christ.
- She knows Him, He knows her, and they relate well to each other.
- She possesses gifts of the Spirit that I do not have.

The things the Spirit has given to me are not identical to what He has given to her, which is why I do not see her as an "irritating appendage to our marriage." Lucia is an instrumental asset to what the Lord is doing in our lives. She is my most valuable ally, and I trust her walk with God and the wisdom that He gives her. I want to know what she is hearing from the Lord.

- Does your spouse have a relationship with God?
- Are you willing to tap into that relationship and learn what God is revealing to your partner?
- Are you willing to accept the possibility that God may be leading your spouse in the right decision?
- Are you more about being right, or are you more about discerning God's perspective regardless of who came up with the idea?

The Wife Is Not a Doormat

The wife can and should make a humble appeal to her husband when she believes—in her conscience—that her husband may be making a poor decision. There is no such teaching in Scripture that a wife is to submit to her husband in everything, though some misinterpret the "everything" in Ephesians 5:24.

(For example, if your husband asked you to kill your son, you would not submit to his request. Perhaps he asks you to lie, cheat, or steal. In any of those cases, your allegiance to the Lord would forbid you from submitting to your husband. Having a sound hermeneutic is critical when interpreting Bible words, verses, passages, meanings, and contexts.)

A wife is to submit to her husband. And she should be humble and respectful toward her husband, but I have told my wife many times that if she does not share what she thinks, she is not serving me effectively or honoring God completely. I do not want a doormat wife. I do not want her to agree with me just because it may be the path of least resistance. I want a wife who can boldly appeal but yet humbly submit to me. I want a wife who can think for herself.

Of course, it's incumbent upon me to create a context of grace where she experiences the freedom to speak her mind according to how she is hearing from God. I need my wife to complement me (Genesis 2:18). We need each other.

- Husband, how have you created a context of grace in your home that motivates your wife to share her authentic thoughts?
- How do you hinder her from being free within the marriage to share openly, honestly, and transparently?
- Wife, are you willing to step up courageously and serve your husband and honor God by appealing to him according to how God is leading you?
- Do you respect your husband?

It's Not about the Decision

When decisions divide, there is something wrong with the marriage. The marriage is a one-flesh union that nothing splits except death, which is why decision-making is a beautiful opportunity to assess your relationship with each other. Decisions are opportunities to put Christ on display in your marriage.

If you do not make Christ your centerpiece because of childishness, fighting, and pettiness, the decision you're attempting to make becomes a mirror that shows the exact condition of your relationship. If your marriage cannot withstand the decision-making process or the outcome of the decisions that you make, you need to find help because there is something wrong with your relationship. There is nothing that should disrupt continuously the unity and harmony found in the marriage union. The husband and wife are a picture of Christ and His church (Ephesians 5:21–33).

- What does your decision-making process typically reveal about your marriage?
- Are you a cohesive team, a divided couple, or somewhere in the middle?
- Do you look forward to tackling problems together?
- What do you need to change to become better partners in the decision-making process?

The Gospel Drives Decision-Making

A couple who rightly understands the gospel realizes that Christ resolved their most significant decision at the cross. There is nothing they will ever face that will come close to the problem they had at the cross. Because of this gospel reality, a couple interacts with each other as grateful friends who see all of life as a gift. This couple is not controlled by what they get or do not get because they live in the daily awareness of getting far better than they deserve.

Their pressing desires do not dictate or drive them. They live in the daily contentment that Christ offers through the gospel. Gratitude characterizes them now. It is no longer about wins or losses. Their ambitions are for the glory of God, not for personal gain or glory-robbing. They will accept a "no" just as easily as they accept a "yes." It's not about either one but rather about accomplishing God's will in their relationship.

There is no tug-o-war between them, but rather they are two people pulling the same direction. They are mutually cheering for each other while living in the daily amazement of the gospel. This kind of couple is each seeking the interests of the other (Matthew 22:36–40).

"Do nothing from selfish ambition or conceit, but in humility count others more significant than yourselves. Let each of you look not only to his own interests but also to the interests of others" (Philippians 2:3–4).

- How does the gospel affect your spouse in the decision-making process?
- How does it affect you?
- Do you have to win, regardless of the outcome? Why or why not?
- Are you genuinely seeking to accept your spouse's position?
- Is your first instinct to find the good in your spouse's point of view?

I have given you more than two dozen questions to ponder. Will you permit these questions to be your marital homework assignment over the next couple of weeks? Perhaps you can go on a few dates to discuss what you've just read.

Chapter 21

Relationship Endurance

"Men Wanted – For hazardous journey. Small wages, bitter cold, long months of complete darkness, constant danger, safe return doubtful. Honor and recognition in case of success." — Ernest Shackleton

"Others suffered mocking and flogging, and even chains and imprisonment. They were stoned, they were sawn in two, they were killed with the sword. They went about in skins of sheep and goats, destitute, afflicted, mistreated—of whom the world was not worthy—wandering about in deserts and mountains, and in dens and caves of the earth" (Hebrews 11:36–38).

Ernest Shackleton was an explorer during the early part of the 20th century. He made three expeditions to the Antarctic. The quote was his way of recruiting men for his most dangerous journey. The second quote is one of the many Bible warnings of what you are getting yourself into if you choose to follow Christ. The call to live the Christian life is a call to die. When you were born a second time (John 3:7), God gave you two gifts. The first gift was salvation, and the second gift was suffering.

"For it has been granted to you that for the sake of Christ you should not only believe in him but also suffer for his sake" (Philippians 1:29).

Christ, like Shackleton, did not hide the truth about His mission. Plain, direct, and honest. He did not sugarcoat what it meant to follow Him (1 Peter 2:21). There has always been a death feel to the Christian experience.

"Then Jesus told his disciples, 'If anyone would come after me, let him deny himself and take up his cross and follow me. For whoever would save his life will lose it, but whoever loses his life for my sake will find it'" (Matthew 16:24–25).

Typically, when a person enters into a relationship with Christ, they are full of hope and confidence, assuming there will be good times ahead. And there are. How could it be otherwise? To walk with Christ is to walk in victory, and the early days of the Christian experience are like a date with a fantastic girl. It is fun and carefree, until a year later after you marry her and bring her home to live with for the rest of your life. Dating is fun. Marriage is a call to die.

As the new Christian continues the journey, he begins to realize how things are more complex and challenging than what he first imagined. Along with this realization is the temptation to shrink back from his calling to follow Jesus (Matthew 19:16–26). The temptation to quit when things become hard is a typical human experience. Relational exits are appealing when the relationship becomes difficult. Whenever you place two sinners in proximity to each other for an extended period, there will be a temptation to sever, quit, and leave the relationship.

It is impossible to avoid relational conflict, whether the issue is with God or someone else. The faith you had when you began the relationship will wane during the relationship. Your confidence will erode. Whether it is your new faith, new job, or new wife, the process is the same. Every relationship begins with the hope and expectation of good things to come, and then stuff happens. The things you liked about the person are overpowered and overshadowed by the things that tear away at the fabric of the union.

Suffering Produces Endurance

- Did you know that suffering in our world is a component of relationship building?
- Did you know that the ability to endure situational difficulties between two people is an essential ingredient for relational success?
- Did you know that endurance is distinctive of the Christian life?

Endurance is a grace gift from the Lord. He gives this gift to His children, not just to survive the relationship but to mature through the relationship. Notice how Paul thought about the role of endurance in our suffering. Follow his equation: suffering produces endurance.

"Not only that, but we rejoice in our sufferings, knowing that suffering produces endurance, and endurance produces character, and character produces hope, and hope does not put us to shame, because God's love has been poured into our hearts through the Holy Spirit who has been given to us" (Romans 5:3–4).

Endurance grows out of suffering. Whether you are training for a marathon or a marriage, you will not learn endurance without prerequisite suffering. No suffering; no endurance. One may say, "If endurance comes from suffering, I don't want to endure." That may sound reasonable on the surface, but it is problematic because suffering is part of every human's experience. Nobody gets a pass from suffering because suffering is a promise from God (Genesis 3:8–18).

You do not get to choose whether you want to suffer. The mature Christian not only understands this but engages suffering from hope, knowing Christlike character begins its formation in the crucible of difficulties. Your most satisfying relationships will be the ones you endured, not the ones you severed because the way became hard for you. This perspective makes endurance an essential element to have fulfilling relationships. This challenge does not come effortlessly or without a fight, and it is not a foregone conclusion that you will endure. The temptation to shrink back from the hardness of life is natural because the challenges within relationships are harder to navigate than any of us can imagine.

The Key to Endurance

"Therefore do not throw away your confidence, which has a great reward. For you have need of endurance, so that when you have done the will of God you may receive what is promised" (Hebrews 10:35–36).

There is a race set before you, and you need the endurance to succeed. Your temptation (and mine, too) will be to throw away the relationship when it becomes hard.

"Let us also lay aside every weight, and sin which clings so closely, and let us run with endurance the race that is set before us" (Hebrews 12:1b).

Self-Analysis

• How do I gain the endurance needed to persevere in a relationship?

- What is the one essential element that will keep me focused on the prize of a satisfying relationship?

Our clues to these questions are found in the mystery to endurance in the Hebrew writer's final thoughts in chapter ten, just before he launches into the faith chapter. He clearly states to his readers why they were able to endure terrible hardships and situational difficulties.

"For you had compassion on those in prison, and you joyfully accepted the plundering of your property, since you knew that you yourselves had a better possession and an abiding one" (Hebrews 10:34).

The reason they endured was because of what they knew. It might be better to say who they knew. Though they did not know all the reasons why they were going through conflict, they did know who was with them in the conflict. Though they were not getting all of their questions answered, they were aware of how there was something that transcended their unanswered questions. They knew God, and their knowledge of Him was enough to stabilize their souls during the difficulties they were experiencing. When Rick Warren preached his first message after the suicide of his son, he had a long time to process one of the most painful experiences a human could ever endure. Two of the things he said in that message were:

- What you know is what gets you through.
- There is no growth without change; there is no change without loss; there is no loss without pain; and there is no pain without grief.

Stewarding Your Pain

Warren discerned a transcending piece of the Christian puzzle: he found God to be higher than the fear that was in his soul. For years he had prayed, asking God for answers and help regarding his son. In the end, his son took his life. This shock left Rick and Kay in an unresolvable situation—his son was not coming back to them. His soul struggle highlighted one of the elements of mystery in the frustrations of life. No matter how hard you try, there will never be satisfying answers that will adequately explain all you may want to know regarding what is happening to you. Your strength and your sanity will come from what you know to be right about God during the hard times.

What you know about Him is what will get you through your dark times. If you are more aware of God, who is in your trouble, you will be able to endure your difficulty. Knowing or possessing more information about why you are going through what you are going through will not give you the endurance you need. Endurance does not come from knowing all the answers for why you are going through hardship. Endurance comes from knowing God and radically holding on to Him when life hurls the hard times at you. God is weaving His mysterious message into your soul and is calling you to steward His work in your life.

"God wants to take your greatest pain and turn it into your life's message." —Rick Warren

The gospel was the worst thing that happened to Jesus because to fulfill the gospel meant He had to die. His most significant and most excruciating pain became His life's message. It was through His endurance that we could receive eternal life, and you have a similar opportunity to turn your greatest pain into your life's message. God is calling you to gospel-motivated and gospel-centered suffering by using your pain as a message to help others. Properly stewarding your pain will happen if what you know and Who you know is more significant than your problems.

Christians who can endure hardships spend more time thinking about God than their problems. Problem-centered Christians will not endure. They want what they are not getting more than they want God to work through their suffering. Christ had a similar temptation. He was shrinking back in the garden of Gethsemane (Luke 22:42). He was losing endurance. For a moment, it appeared as if He was not going to make it to the cross. The gospel seemed lost in the garden. Then He refocused and submitted Himself to His Father's will rather than to His own wants.

Call to Action

- Do you talk more about your problems or God who is in your problems?
- Whose will are you looking to proclaim during your suffering?
- Do you see how your suffering can fuel endurance and how endurance can give you Christlike character?
- Will you pray right now, asking the Father to give you the grace gift of endurance?

Suffering produces endurance and endurance produces character. You will know when sound Christian character is formed in you by how you think about God and others through your suffering. When your greatest joy is to serve God and others (Matthew 22:36–40) more than serving yourself (Philippians 2:3–4), you will have the endurance you need to endure the race that is before you. When your deep confidence in your future with Christ is what you know and what you believe, you will be able to endure any hardship. This kind of faith comes from Christ, the One who endured the worst hardships for our benefit.

"For the joy that was set before him endured the cross, despising the shame, and is seated at the right hand of the throne of God" (Hebrews 12:2).

Christ kept the end in mind. His deep confidence in what the Father was going to accomplish through Him steadied His soul as He poured out His life on earth. He knew whom He believed and would not deviate from His knowledge of God, no matter how hard things became. If you lack endurance, there is something about your suffering in which you have not come to terms. If you lack endurance, there is something you want more than God. Endurance comes somewhere between suffering and character. It is the bridge that connects the two. The way you cross that bridge is by wanting Christ more than anything else in this world.

It is possible that your life is in a good place right now because you're dating, happy, and about to get married. It would be wise to bookmark this chapter because after you get married, life will go places that you never imagined, and some of those doors you walk through will have "suffering" written over it. This chapter may be the most important one in this book.

Chapter 22

A Blessed Relationship

When Biff and Mable were married, they appeared to be the perfect pair. They were high school sweethearts and were virtually inseparable. They went to the same church and kept themselves pure throughout their courtship. After marriage, Biff went into the ministry, and Mable was excited to be married to her "preacher man." They were best friends who enjoyed doing things together.

Then life happened.

Initially, it was their jobs. Then came the bills. There were a couple of unexpected medical emergencies that set them back, and by year five they had two children. Mable quit her public job to be a mom, which they both agreed was the right thing to do.

They never saw it coming.

By the time the second child arrived, Biff and Mable had already drifted apart. They were civil to each other, but the marriage had evolved into a business partnership rather than a spiritually dynamic relationship.

Biff and Mable's scenario can happen to any couple in today's culture. It's called, "life happens." The bad news is that when life does happen, couples do not know how to adjust. They don't know how to respond to each other, and, more importantly, they do not know how to respond to God.

Being a Christian is not all you need to have satisfying relationships if your Christianity does not connect you deeply with God and others. The Christian experience is spiritual first and functional second. If you're not connected spiritually, your function will be religion and nothing more.

Assumed Relationship with God

One of the things I've seen with Christian couples is an assumed relationship with God. The husband assumes his wife has a relationship with God. The wife believes her husband has a relationship with God. Neither one of them is actively involved in each other's spiritual lives, even though they both attend separate Bible studies and rarely miss their local church meetings. These Christian activities have become nothing more than feel-good social gatherings with a sprinkling of Bible on top.

Biff and Mable made no plans to become spiritually intrusive with each other or with their friends. This case study represents some of the most common patterns for people with marriage problems that end in divorce. There is an appearance of sanctification, but, in truth, it is more like group-participation in the customs of religion that has no transformative power.

Being transparent and vulnerable about their true selves is hard for them. They do not have this kind of relationship with each other or with their friends. Though Mable has been more honest with her friends, she is not married to them. She is one flesh with Biff. No matter how much she is invigorated by being with her friends, she has a disease in her one-flesh body. Her relationship with her friends only highlights the problems in her marriage as they remind her of what she is missing.

Pursuing Threefold Unity

If they want to transform their relationship, Biff, Mable, and God must do more than coexist in a superficial threefold relationship. Merely attending more church services or participating in additional Bible studies will not work. Their primary problem is not about the church or the Bible. The issue in view here is about a couple and the Lord and the shallow way in which they relate to each other. The church and the Bible can facilitate their spiritual relationship, but their problem is that they don't have a spiritual relationship with each other. Only when they revive the spiritual dysfunction in their one-flesh union will the church and the Bible be able to help them.

At this point, the church and the Bible are like pouring water on a duck's back. You have to change the duck so that it can absorb the water. Biff and Mable have to change to receive the ongoing and mutual benefit of the many "means of grace" that can help them to mature into a God-centered, one-flesh union. This change begins with a spiritual transformation of their hearts because they are spiritual beings. A spiritual being created them in His image. God designed them to relate to Him and each other spiritually. This type of community is how the first couple functioned (Genesis 2:18–25). It was when Adam and Eve decided to break-up their trifold relationship with God that things went wrong for them (Genesis 3:1–15).

The missing piece that will kill any marriage is when God, the husband, and the wife are not dynamically involved with each other in a deeply committed, spiritual way. This spiritual malfunction is what happened to Biff and Mable. The busyness of home life and the ministry put them on a path that sucked the spiritual sustenance out of them. They never saw it coming because they were "in the ministry," as though the ministry insulates a couple from trouble. In time, they were doing ministry by rote rather than by relationship. It was a "form of Christianity" that was devoid of the power they needed to keep them spiritually in tune with God and each other. Their trifold relationship began to drift from each other.

Diagnosing the Triangle

It is a simple matter to diagnose a broken marriage. You only have to ask a few questions to get at the heart of what has gone wrong between a couple and the Lord. Here are five straightforward queries that you can use to assess your marriage as well as the marriages of your friends. The answers to these questions will give you an accurate picture of how a marriage is thriving. With each question, provide specific and detailed responses. Avoid Christian-speak and ambiguity. Focus more on being practical rather than theoretical. Above all, be honest.

- Husband, describe your relationship with the Lord.
- Wife, describe your relationship with the Lord.
- Both of you describe your marital relationship with the Lord.
- Husband, describe your involvement with your wife's relationship with the Lord.
- Wife, describe your involvement with your husband's relationship with the Lord.

Your answers will reveal your spiritual interest and intentionality with the Lord and with your spouse. The questions go beyond the activities that you do together, the jobs you have, or the respective events you engage in with each other. Your answers should not be, "We go to church together." I've already addressed the problem with "going to church" while having a spiritually distant relationship with each other and God. These questions are spiritual. They represent the foundation of your marriage—the most critical aspect of your life. How you answer them will determine the quality of your relationship and whether you will be able to persevere as a married couple joyfully.

These questions reveal the systemic core to all marriage problems. If a couple has communication problems, it means there is something broken in their spiritual lives. If a couple has financial issues, it says there is something afoul at the level of their hearts. You name the problem in any marriage, and you can trace it back to its core—the couple's trifold relationship with God. If you fix this core problem, which is spiritual, you'll be able to resolve all of the other issues in the marriage.

Rebuilding Your Relationship

Once the man's wonderfulness begins to wear off or the wife's beauty begins to fade, you'll have to find something else to be excited about in the relationship. The culture's solution for this is to make more money so that they can spend it on themselves. They present a pretense of happiness, but they are not happy. Biff and Mable are scrambling to figure out how to replace God with something else in their lives. Some Christians attempt to replace God with their jobs, children, and cultural hobbies. Biff and Mable used the ministry, though they did not see it that way.

The ministry is a more sanitized solution and gives the perception of being right with God and each other, but a marriage can still rot from the pulpit or the front row. The reason this was the case for Biff and Mable was that they did not know how to have a triangulated relationship with each other and God. What might surprise you is how simple it is to have this kind of relationship. The catch is that both partners must be willing to humble themselves to put forth the effort to love each other the way God intends. Many times my initial counsel to a couple like this is as simple as praying together. The way I present this idea to them goes like this: "I want you both to go home, and at some point today, I want you both to sit on your bed, hold hands, and begin talking to God."

It is straightforward counsel, and if a couple chose to humble themselves, they would see God do some remarkable things in their lives (James 4:6). What they would be doing is building a triangulated relationship between themselves and God. Because their problems are primarily matters of the heart, they must work on their issues at that level. Spiritual problems need more than partial or shallow solutions. One couple told me how they were counseled to mirror each other. Mirroring is a counseling technique where one spouse reflects what the other spouse is saying to enhance their communication. Ironically, as they were telling me about mirroring, they started arguing.

Why were they arguing? They don't like each other. There were layers of unforgiveness, bitterness, hurt, resentment, harshness, grudges, and disappointment in their lives. These are spiritual (heart-related) issues. While communication techniques can help, they won't resolve the core problems until the couple addresses their spiritual issues. Unforgiveness, bitterness, hurt, resentment, harshness, grudges, and disappointment can only be rooted out with the Spirit's intervention.

Expose the Heart

This process means they must have God's solutions more than they need man-centered communication techniques. Until God implodes these spiritual problems, there will be no technique that will work for them. It's like trying to paint over a stain. It won't work. You must remove the stain. The simple act of sitting on the bed, holding hands, and talking to God is a practical first step in breaking the bondage that has been crippling their marriage. Think about what would be involved in doing this simple task.

Humility – First of all the couple would have to humble themselves. Resisting pride is usually the hardest part for individuals. As they humble themselves before the Lord and each other, their sin will become exposed.

Transparency – Their humility will lead them toward openness. Being open and honest with each other will be new for the couple. It will feel mechanical or wooden because it's not Biff and Mable's habit. In the past, they were defending their positions.

Vulnerability – Humble transparency has an element of weakness. Up to this point, the couple has been unwilling to let down their guards. Now they are laying their weapons down and rather than seeking their interests, Biff and Mable are looking to the benefit of the other (Philippians 2:3–4).

Rather than demanding personal rights, they are attempting to model the gospel (Philippians 2:5–7). You begin to sense a tonal difference in their relationship. They begin to sound and talk differently. Humility, transparency, and vulnerability are far different from their former, punitive demands.

Intimacy – This simple act of prayer has another element, too —they are holding hands. This physical activity is an intimate act. Physical intimacy has been missing in their relationship. They are now willing to take baby steps with the hope of restoring not just the spiritual brokenness but the physical brokenness as well. Much resentment can vanish with the touch of the hand. I recommend to couples that they practice hand-holding as well as putting their arms around each other. It seems rare for couples in their forties and beyond to hold hands or sit with their arms around each other and show public affection.

Prayer Works

Prayer – There is one more element to this simple act of praying together, which is the most crucial aspect of all: they are talking to God. Before they were talking to each other in aggravated tones or maybe they were implementing the silent treatment. Now, rather than distancing themselves from each other and God, they are choosing to build a threefold relationship together. In time, they can enjoy a spiritually dynamic relationship with each other and God.

- Take a look at these words: humility, transparency, vulnerability, intimacy, and prayer.
- Take a look at these words: demands, resentment, disappointment, unforgiveness, and hurt.

The first group of words sits upon a spiritually, dynamic, triangulated relationship between God, a husband, and a wife. The second group of words is devoid of God while leaving the couple in a Darwinian survival-of-the-fittest, loser-leaves-town match. One of the best things a broken couple can do is to pray together actively. Praying together removes the walls that divide. As they begin to build their relationship with God and each other, they will be able to address some of the other problems in their marriage.

While this is the first step to a long journey, it is probably the hardest one of all. It takes a lot of humility for two stubborn people to set aside their disappointment for a higher good. If this is you, I appeal for you to take steps to begin developing or rebuilding your relationship from the ground up. At some point today, I want you both to sit on your bed, hold hands, and begin talking to God because your most perfect relationship will be when you, your spouse, and God become one spiritually.

Conclusion

From Dating to Divorce

Marriage counseling is the most common kind of counseling that I do. The reason for this is because marriages are the most common, long-term relationship between two people. Children typically leave home after a couple of decades. Siblings tend to separate from each other as they seek marriage partners and move into their unique adult lives.

Married couples are different: they are in a relationship for the long haul—at least until death separates them. Marriage is an expected fifty plus year context where two sinners come together for better or worse. If you put two sinners in a room (home) for an extended period with no plan for escape, you can expect problems. There may be a lot of love and other satisfying things happening in their lives, but there will also be problems. It's unavoidable.

The dating couple is different. Those lovebirds can break up and go on to the next relationship if things become difficult. Vocational relationships are similar. If you don't like your boss or the environment in which you work, you can move on to the next thing.

Marriage?

Not so.

A relationship that leads to marriage is easy and even fun to get into, but be warned: there is not an escape route from the union, other than death (Matthew 19:8). Sadly, too many couples do create another kind of escape route. It's called divorce. I'm going to walk you through a four-step process that can lead to divorce if you do not apply the things I have been teaching in this book. This sequence is the most common "dating to divorce chronology" that I have encountered during my counseling career.

Number One

- Biff meets Mable.
- Biff likes Mable.

Number Two

- Biff and Mable begin to date.
- Biff and Mable fall in love.
- Biff asks Mable to marry him.
- Mable says, "Yes!"
- Biff and Mable plan a wonderful life together.

Number Three

- Mable gets mad at Biff. Biff gets mad at Mable. The road gets bumpy.
- Mable becomes pregnant.
- Biff starts working extended hours because it's hard to live with Mable.
- Biff deduces that being a provider is better than nothing.
- Biff becomes a "superstar" at his work. Everybody loves Biff.
- Biff flirts with a woman at his job.
- Mable continues to be angry with Biff.
- Mable becomes consumed with her children because it's hard to live with Biff.

- Biff and Mable become preoccupied with life.
- Biff and Mable appear to be the model Christian couple.
- Biff and Mable's children become teenagers, more independent, and spend less time around the house.

Number Four

- Biff and Mable are "forced" to spend more time together in their "emptying nest."
- Biff and Mable still do not like each other. They become even more snippy and unrepentant.
- Biff and Mable get a divorce after twenty-nine years of marriage. Their local church is shocked. People don't understand.

The Artificial Season

One of the most significant problems in this type of marriage is that the couple acts as if their relationship began the day they first met, while not fully considering the kind of people they have always been, especially before they met each other. Every person enters into their dating relationship broken.

- There is brokenness due to the fall of Adam.
- There is brokenness due to the shaping influences of other people and other things.
- There is brokenness due to the choices that they have made.

By the time a person enters into a dating relationship, he (or she) comes into that relationship with baggage. We all have baggage: fallen shaping influences given to us by Adam, others, and ourselves. After you mix your baggage with the baggage of your spouse, there is no way to avoid combustion in the home. Biff and Mable had preexisting baggage before they met. Lots of it. While they were dating, they "sat their luggage aside" and put their best foot forward. While dating, they were determined to be on their best behavior. It's like holding your breath for as long as you can. This problem is why it is usually wise to date at least a year before you pop the question, which is not a mandate from Scripture but a good idea for most couples. A year gives you time to see the other person in more real contexts and relational activity. You can only hold your breath for so long. Eventually, the real person will reveal himself or herself.

Biff would hold the car door open for Mable. He would send her flowers. Biff was always kind, sensitive, and patient, and he loved attending their local church meetings with Mable. I'm not saying he was a total fake, but I am implying that he was not revealing the totality of who he was. I have called the dating season the artificial season where two people fake each other out as much as they can—until after they are married.

Baggage Handling

As you have probably surmised, Biff and Mable are sinners. They not only came from their respective mother's wombs speaking lies, but they created a whole lot of baggage before they met each other. Some of their baggage was their own doing, while the rest of it people heaped upon them. Either way, they both had undealt-with baggage. They did not perceive or resolve all of their issues during their amazing dating relationship. Their premarriage counseling was inadequate. They had no one with courage, grace, wisdom, or competence to speak into their lives. And they were "in love," so there was very little anyone could tell them anyway.

Biff and Mable left their baggage at the dating door and didn't pick it up again until they were six months into their marriage. By then, it was too late—at least for them, because they were too proud to let anyone in on their mutual marriage disappointment.

An Aside – Most of my marriage counseling is either with couples who have been married five years or less or fifteen years or more. That is not an absolute rule, but a general one. If the couple is wise and humble, they will seek help early in their marriage. These spouses will not be like Biff and Mable. They will realize there is something not quite right, and since they are not quite sure the best course of action, they will reach out to their church for help. Then there are those who are married for more than a decade, and they cannot keep it under wraps any longer. Their marriage problems begin to escape their ability to keep it quiet. They start to empty nest when the children become more independent and do not need their parents as much. The couple is without a sin plan, and they are less distracted by their children. This reality leaves them with four options:

- They find help.
- They get a divorce.
- They find other distractions like ministry, hobbies, or grandchildren.
- The coexist in a house that is not a home until one of them dies.

Call to Action

My appeal to any couple in trouble, regardless of the length of your relationship, is to get help. God's grace is more powerful than your problems, no matter how complicated and involved you think your issues are. The Bible has a lot to say about working through conflict. There is a plan for sin, and it begins with the gospel. The only requirement is humility (James 4:6). Though you may have started on the wrong foot, it does not mean you have to stay that way. God came to redeem and restore that which we can't fix. Fixing broken things is at the heart of the gospel. I appeal to you to get help today!

There are more than 250 questions in this book. Each chapter is an opportunity for you to get to work with your dating partner or spouse. Maybe you want to go back to the beginning. Why not? Take your time. Go through it carefully with a competent friend or, better yet, your spouse if you're married. You're not in a sprint, but you must do something. Act now! If you are dating, this book will be transformative as it sets a trajectory for your best possible marriage now.

Are you ready? Let's go.

About the Author

Rick Thomas has been training in the Upstate of South Carolina since 1997. After several years as a counselor and pastor, he founded and launched his training organization to encourage and equip people for effective living.

In the early '90s, he earned a BA in Theology. Later he received a BS in Education. Rick became ordained into Christian ministry in 1993, and in 2000, he graduated with an MA in Counseling. The Association of Certified Biblical Counselors recognized him as a Fellow in 2006. His organization is a certified training center for the International Association of Biblical Counselors where you can receive your certification as a Biblical Counselor.

Today his organization reaches individuals and families in every country through training, blogging, podcasting, counseling, and coaching. His cyber home is RickThomas.Net. He has authored three books.

Join Our Team

Our community is a gathering of individuals from all over the world who are seeking to live more productive and inspiring lives. We all have situational and relational challenges that could benefit from having other people bringing insight and care. Caring for others is what our community does best.

Community Resources

- Access to a stocked library of content written from a God-centered, others-centered perspective
- Live and archived webinars
- Training presentations, videos, infographics, mind maps, best practices, and more
- Private membership-only forum for questions and answers about life and relationships
- Opportunities to ask Rick and his team key questions that are important to you
- A 24/7 all-access "life coach" for personal development and training of others
- An all online, self-paced Mastermind Training Program: Distance Education

Partner with Us

We are a membership-supported community. You can also partner with us by making a one-time or recurring donation. We are a 501(c) 3 NPO. To learn more, go to our ministry website, RickThomas.Net.

Made in the USA
Lexington, KY
08 April 2019